Writer's
Bloc V

Mystic Publishers, Inc
614 Mosswood Dr.
Henderson, NV 89002
www.mysticpublishers.com

Special thanks to our judge,
John D. Barton of Utah State University

For the parents of writers, especially ours.

TABLE OF CONTENTS

Poetry

Nonfiction

Fiction

Teasers

2013 Student Writing Contest Winners

College Level

High School Level

Writer's Bloc V

POETRY

GARRY BUZICK

Garry Buzick lives in Las Vegas, Nevada. Published in
Seeds Literary Magazine, Wedding Bouquet, and *Treasure
Box* (Patchwork Path anthologies), *Writer's Bloc III,* and
Writer's Bloc IV. Available on Amazon, *Throwaways—
Perfect Match,* a paranormal thriller. Contact Garry at
buzickg@yahoo.com.

Adrift

Adrift in the late summer doldrums
Distant shore seemingly impossible
And to what end, beginning or end of journey?
The water of all life laps lazily across my bow
This nameless ship, unworthy of title
No longer sleek, swift or wind driven
Lounging in the sea of self-pity, merely afloat
Deep blue terror, unknown, but somehow inviting
Frozen—hot in the sweltering air, immobile
My plight, my preference, my indifference
Perspiring memories puddle—then plump
Spill slowly over heart, trickle past the lowered mast
Battered by many storms, softened by the raging seas
Sometimes listening for a distant breeze
Neither desiring or demanding, slipping further
Pleasure erased even with a ship full of rum
Worthless gold aplenty without a merchant near
Adrift…

GLORY WADE

Glory Wade writes various genres. She is a member of Henderson Writers' Group and coordinates the Aliante Writers' Group. Her published credentials include short fiction stories; pet-oriented, event planning and jewelry articles; and a chapter in the Professional Meeting Management textbook. She is editing her first novel, *Ashes to Diamonds, Dust to Dust*. A childrens' picture book series about *Folly Dolly the Doxie* is in progress. Contact email: glorywadewriter@gmail.com.

Buckie the Clown

This was written while flying home on May 28, 2005 after visiting my parents. When I cleaned out Dad's car to sell it, the last items I removed were his oversized clown shoes and clown horn from the corner of the trunk. I took them to his office in the basement.

Huge white clown shoes
  scuffed from miles of pavement in parades
  and the dirt of fairgrounds
  and the floors of shopping malls

In these shoes, my Dad walked
  and stood, making animals
  out of balloons
  for throngs of happy children—
  young and old, and in-between

They sit on his office floor now
  in the basement of the house he no longer lives in
  with his funny little horn
  he would honk
  putting smiles on the faces of excited children.

They sit here alone
  never to be worn again—

Dad sits in his room
in a care facility
unable to remember those happy times—
unable to apply his clown makeup
or don his shoes with their oversized bubble toes
that caused him to walk with toes pointed outward
that cause him knee problems now
but also made him happy
and lots of kids laugh
and lots of adults smile

Buckie the Clown, my Dad.
Buckie can't come out any more
but Dad is here—in an Alzheimer's haze—but here
loved now just for himself.
Buckie the Clown no more.

NONFICTION

JENNY BALLIF

Jenny has worked as a wildland firefighter, doula, and childbirth educator. She lives in southern Nevada with her husband and their three kids. Her memoir, *Cancer of the Mind*, is the story of her journey through Hodgkin's Lymphoma and postpartum depression. *Cockroach Cure*, her first novel, is currently in its second draft. One of Jenny's life long dreams is to become fluent in multiple languages. Given the choice between a six-figure advance and a Spanish-immersion summer abroad with her family in Cuba, she'd pick Cuba.

Essentially Invisible

Mundane is not meaningless, and repetitive is not boring. Mothering young children is often mundane, and always repetitive, but the dishes, diapers, kisses, and giggles of my daily routine are full of meaning and challenge.

It's a life that sometimes feels invisible. So much of my time is spent indoors in the company of two little persons who aren't much taller than my knees. So many of my actions are erased by time, washed away as quickly as I form them, like I'm a painter using the sand by the surf for a canvas. From time to time, I want to shout that I am doing the most important things. I am absolutely essential.

To mother well is a supreme art, and today I decide I make my symphony visible. Not just for me, but for my husband as well. I'll mark each act with a pink sticky note, and when he gets home, I'll watch with delight as he searches for these bright squares of paper, reads them and discovers the complexity and layers of my day, the musical variety of notes that I've orchestrated to make our house a happy home.

Annabelle runs to me with a squeal, landing on my right foot and twisting her arms and legs firmly around my calf. I shift my laundry basket to the other hip and continue down the hall like a peg-legged pirate, dragging a giggling toddler with every other step.

With one leg still twenty pounds heavier than the other, I manage to get the clothes in the drier. In my mind, I see a pink square of bright paper: Did laundry.

Soon, the upstairs is covered with similar imaginary notes, coupled with imaginary praise from Serge: Clean socks, matched and folded? Wow!

Andrew, my energetic three-year-old, jabs me in the back with a book. "Read it?" We sit together, my voice fills the air with the cadence of rhyme. As soon as one book is done, he bounces off the floor like a drop of water on a hot skillet, running to get another book before Mom can give her attention to something else. Annabelle joins us, and after a dozen or so books, I tickle them both, then turn on all fours and crawl after them, chasing them to their room. They shriek and giggle at my growls, and within a few minutes, they're absorbed in the process of deconstructing their toy closet.

Cleaned toilet. Mopped bathroom floors.

Picked up all the toys.

Breakfast dishes washed and put away.

Made lunch.

More laundry.

My hands take the mass of bread dough and lump it on the counter. My two shadows are there in an instant, pushing chairs up to the counter. "Can I have some dough? Please, please?" I portion off small pinches while shaping the dough into loaves, then cover the pans with a cloth.

When I wash the mixing bowl, Tweedledum and Tweedledee pull every pot and pan from the cupboard, find a few long-handled spoons, and delight themselves with a chorus of loud noise. "Look, Mom, we're cooking!"

"Good job."

Andrew holds out a spoon. "Taste it."

I take a pretend nibble. "Ummm. Delicious. What is it?"

His eyes twinkle as he shouts, "Spicy garlic!"

They double up with laughter when I pretend to spit it out.

Made bread.

Put away pots and pans (every single one of them).

I shepherd my little duo upstairs. "Who wants to help me put away laundry?" I ask. They disappear, vanishing like

ghosts to the next room. After a long moment of silence—
it's too quiet—I go to investigate. Every blanket, pillow, and
soft toy in their room is piled together on the floor.

"Look, Mom! We made a plumpy plump."

Soon the blankets and pillows from my own bed are
missing.

"Nap time!" I tell my jumping beans, who protest loudly,
telling me they need just one more, no, just five more jumps
onto the plumpy plump. We count down jumps, then I
wrangle their energetic little selves through the nap routine:
stories, drink of water, lie down.

"Be quiet."

"Lie down"

"Hey, I said, lie down."

"Get back in bed now, or else!"

Suddenly, they're unconscious, so placid and still it's
hard to believe they ever lived in a state other than this,
angels dreaming. I settle down on the couch with a book.

Made all the beds, twice.

Cleaned up lunch.

Dinner time approaches. I work at the stove while my
defenders of entropy wage a steady campaign in the front
room, taking all the children's books out of the bookshelf.
I think of my day, and the dozens of bright post-it notes I
could stick up all over the house. I'm amazing, I tell myself.
I have the most wonderful, important job, and I'm good at it.
But there's no time to write notes, the sink is again cluttered
with dirty dishes, despite the fact that I washed dishes two,
no—three times today.

If I did have time, I would put a note on the back of each
kid saying, "Mom carried, diapered, fed, and loved me, all
day long. She met all my needs and discerned which of my
wants should be met, and how (no small task!)."

And on my own back, I could put a little note saying, "I
spent one hour relaxing and reading a book." I plan to tell
Serge all about my imaginary notes when he gets home, to
impress him with my heroics, with all the important and

beautiful things I did today. I'm contemplating the number and volume of these notes when the door opens. Serge is home from work.

We smile and exchange hugs, then the two little ones run at him, their arms point up, reaching with energetic desperation. "Daddy, Daddy! Pick me up! Daddy!"

Through the noise I ask, "Do you know what I was going to do today, but didn't, I ran out of time?"

Serge wrinkles his forehead and looks from side to side. I see his eyes pass over the sink. With a shrug, he gives his guess, "The dishes?"

TONI PACINI

Southern Gothic Author, Craftswoman, and Storyteller. Toni Pacini's stories piled up throughout a bizarre life that began in a small cotton mill village in Alabama. Fervently instructed not to "ever tell," she speaks out in her recently completed memoir, *Alabama Blue*, and has burst forth into the second half of her life with words flowing freely.

2004-2006, Toni honed her skills as a member of South Bay Writers Group where an excerpt from *Alabama Blue*, titled "Pepperell Lake", was published in the group's anthology.

2007 in California, Toni ran Sanger Open-Mic Group, served as Vice-President of Sanger Woman's Club, won honors for her writing, and had several local interest articles published in local newspapers and Kings River Life's online magazine.

Toni had a total of five shorts in the March 2013 and July 2013 issues of Bella Online Literary Review's *Mused*. She now resides in Las Vegas, Nevada.

Grandpa Snake-Eyes

Grandpa, 1904-1974

Grandpa Aldridge was a heavy drinker in the days before the cancer. While still able to work, he smoked, drank, and raised hell. Most of the hell he raised was directed toward his family. This created secrets that my grandparents insisted never be shared outside of our home.

"Don't let the neighbors know. Never tell."

A big part of Grandma's purpose was cleaning up after Grandpa's tirades so no one would know what went on inside our thin walls. It was not an uncommon occurrence for Grandma to have to take a long, cane pole, designed especially for this purpose with a scoop on the end, and fish Grandpa's teeth out of the outhouse hole after he lost his dentures, along with his cookies, the night before. Maybe, it was because Grandma's father was a raging drunk, too, that she seemed to accept such duties as part of being a wife.

Grandpa had been adopted, and I never heard much of his history. His birth name was Oliver Sullivan Aldridge. He looked Irish, and he said he was, but his surname, Aldridge, is a Sax name. The majority of Aldridge's I researched came from Wales, another mystery.

No one talked about race when I was a child. Anyone who wasn't a pure white Protestant was a heathen sinner or a foreigner to be watched. Of course, most of those pure white Protestants were at least part Native American, who were called Indians when I was a child, or African American—I won't say what they were called, or Polish, Greek, Italian, or—fill in the blank—Americans. However, no one would admit their true blood, their heritage, because of well-placed fears of discrimination.

The last names and faces told the story, yet no one spoke the truth. Working in the mill and living in the village automatically labeled us as white trash. So the dirty laundry and our personal roots stayed buried in shame at the bottom of an invisible, well-guarded closet. So much so that my siblings and I grew up not really being sure of our own true heritage and nationality.

What a sad society that makes one's roots a source of shame. Our lives were built on generation after generation of shame. How the "telling" heals. That's why I sit at my keyboard tonight, the eve of Thanksgiving, alone, lost in the telling. Grandma couldn't tell; she just kept cleaning. Momma could never tell. She just kept drinking.

Snake-Eyes

I can still smell him, a combination of Old Spice mixed with the pungent aroma of chewing tobacco. Grandpa took a bath every Saturday, whether he needed it or not, and it was always a major production. He had a way of dramatizing everything, and after a performance or the telling of a tale, he always concluded by saying, "Snake-Eyes." No one knows why.

He quit drinking alcohol and smoking cigarettes on July 26, 1950, the day the doctors removed one of his lungs due to cancer. That same day Grandma gladly retired her cane pole, no longer needing to rescue Grandpa's dentures from the outhouse. Absent the booze, it soon became clear to everyone, except Grandpa, that he had been self-medicating a serious mental problem. Years later, after bizarre episodes where he would accuse my grandmother of having affairs with the mailman and the paperboy, Grandpa was diagnosed as a paranoid-schizophrenic.

After Grandpa's lung was removed, he spent the rest of his life dying. I cannot remember the passing of any holiday, or anyone's birthday that he did not announce with sincere reverence, "I ain't gonna be here this time next year."

Yet, he lived for almost twenty-five years after his surgery. I can still see him sitting in his chair, his pocketknife—which had a bone overlay handle, yellowed by age—in one hand and a square of Red Bull tobacco in the other. He would cut off a plug and plop it into his mouth. He was never far from the sweet pea can he used as a portable spittoon. His face was very wrinkled, and the tobacco juice would collect in tiny rivulets at the corners of his mouth.

Grandpa always had a pocketful of toilet paper, and to pass the time, he would entertain himself as well as us kids by rolling tiny squares of paper like mini tusks and horns and stick them in his ears, nose, and mouth, a poor man's origami. Once when a young girl from the village was visiting me, Grandpa couldn't help himself—he loved a new audience—and so he had paper sticking out all over. Angie already found this as odd as I found it embarrassing. Then for his grand finale, Grandpa stuck out his tobacco juice-covered dentures, and little Angie ran home in terror and would never come into our house again. Grandpa roared with laughter; he thought it was hilarious. I did not.

Almost daily he would walk the quarter mile down the highway to Dubois' Service Station. Since the removal of his lung, Grandpa walked bent and hunchbacked. He appeared to be walking against a harsh wind. He would sit with his friends on a bench in front of the station for hours. The ground around the old men's feet and the tops of their shoes would be covered with tiny wood shavings. Some pieces were blonde or almost white; others were a variety of reds and browns. Whittling small pieces of wood with their pocketknives kept their hands busy and gave them an excuse not to look at each other as they talked.

Grandpa sat there all morning till he had to get home for lunch or risk catching hell from Grandma. He spent hours gossiping with the other men who were too sick or old to go into the mill, anymore. They heatedly debated politics, religion, and anything else that came up. Momma called that bench, "The dead peter bench." Now, that was funny.

The Ceiling Fairy

One of my few fond memories of Grandpa was when he would have me sit on his lap while he told me the story of the fairy that lived in a little hole in the corner of our living room ceiling. He told me to look at the hole and concentrate really, really hard, and I might get to see her. I would. I would concentrate so hard while watching for the arrival of the fairy, so focused on that little hole in the ceiling, that when all of a sudden candies would fall from the heavens, I would jump, startled from my concentration. I'd slide off Grandpa's lap and run around the small room gathering my special presents from the fairy. When I got old enough, I caught Grandpa tossing the candies with his right hand while distracting me with his left.

Grandpa's only household responsibility was washing the dinner dishes. He would ceremoniously put on the long, white apron that fell below his knees and fill the two speckled and chipped enamel bowls in the sink, one to wash the dishes and one to rinse. If he were in a good mood, he would sing, when he wasn't talking to himself. Grandpa often made up his own silly little ditties, a habit I inherited. His favorite song was "Adam and Eve in the Garden," which he did not make up, although I have never heard it anywhere except from his lips. It went like this:

Adam and Eve in the garden when the world was very new.

The earth just contained two, and dressmakers very few.

Now, Adam said to Eve in the garden, I have a dandy scheme for you.

When autumn comes, I'll tell you what we'll do.

You'll wear a tulip, a big yellow tulip, and I'll wear a big red rose.

And in Adam's expressing, you could tell by assessing
That he had invented clothes.
Now all the girls in the city were all very pretty,
They each had a smile that glowed.
But if the styles keep on daring all the girls will be wearing—is a smile and a great big rose.
And, as always, Grandpa concluded his performance with, "Snake-Eyes!"

Family Secrets

We always traveled on a clear day in spring or summer because Grandpa wouldn't drive any further than Piggly Wiggly in winter or during bad weather. If the sky were clear and the right time of year, we would all load up in Old Betsy and head off to visit some relative or the other. Grandpa called every car he ever owned "Old Betsy," and he would talk to her up and down the road like she really understood him. He would pat the dashboard or the steering wheel with affectionate encouragement, as you might do with a stubborn horse balking at crossing a stream, and say, "Come on Old Betsy, be a good ole girl; there ya go, that's my girl."

Grandma would pack bologna, deviled ham, or pimento cheese sandwiches on white bread wrapped in waxed paper and potato salad. Or, maybe, fried chicken and her "special fixin's," my favorite being deviled eggs. We would stop somewhere along the way on the side of the road to eat, pee, and rest.

Grandpa was an awful driver, tense and eager to blame others if he made an error. His passengers always sat quietly clinging to the door handles, afraid to speak or even cough. He drove so slowly that we could watch a bug crawl up a fence post as we passed it.

There were no freeways, just old, rutted highways and back roads lined with dust-covered trees and endless miles of kudzu. The towns we drove through were usually no more than a water tower, a stretch of railroad track, and a church.

These tiny towns that awakened us from our road-trip induced trances and prompted us to sit up straight and stare, unwilling as we were to risk missing anything that might be interesting, were all old and poor and looked tired to the bone. No one had air-conditioners in their homes, and certainly not in their automobiles. So, on these little trips, we had no choice other than to keep the windows rolled down and breathe the exhaust along with the bugs. By the time we reached our destination, we were all irritable, hot, sticky, exhausted, and covered with a fine layer of red road dust.

In the spring of 1961, I found myself wedged in between my momma and Uncle Jimmy in the backseat of Old Betsy. We were on our way to visit relatives in Tallassee, which in itself wasn't so bad, but I dreaded seeing Uncle Frank, my Grandpa's older brother. Whenever we went to see him or he visited us, he and Grandpa would sit on the front porch and argue at the top of their lungs—in Grandpa's case, lung—about their views of God and their personal and often disturbing interpretations of the Bible.

A Baptist preacher, Uncle Frank considered himself divinely appointed. His conversations were always riddled with endless references to Hell, the righteous wrath of God, divine punishment, damnation, Satan, demons, and other fear based gibberish. Momma hated Uncle Frank, and she made little effort to be civil, only enough so to keep Grandma and Grandpa off her back. My sister and I instinctively tried to avoid Uncle Frank. We couldn't understand or explain our feelings when we were young, but he always felt "yucky" and frightened us.

Just after my ninth birthday I overheard a conversation that explained a lot. Apparently, the Baptist church had defrocked Uncle Frank many years before when a parishioner caught him raping a black woman in the church. He had hired her to clean, and once he had her powerless and alone in the church, a place that should depict safety, he brutally raped her. Of course, no legal action was taken. In that time and place, a woman would have no justice in such a matter, especially a black woman. Charges would sooner have been brought against Uncle Frank if he had raped Billy Joe Bob's prize winning huntin' dog.

Although defrocked, Uncle Frank continued to call himself Reverend Aldridge until the day he died. Many years later, with the assistance of extensive therapy, I began to piece together the bits of information in my scattered mind files and understand Momma's intense hatred for Uncle Frank.

In hindsight, I can see clearly the classic incest survivor traits that permeated my mother's life: anorexia, depression, self-abuse, and a deep-seeded distrust and disgust for men as a whole. Years ago, Yoko Ono sang and recorded a song written by John Lennon, "Woman is the Nigger of the World." She got that right.

Branches

My grandmother's name was Olemenell Hughey—everyone called her Nell. Grandma had four sisters and one brother: Clementine, Kate, Irene, Tiny, and Fred. I never knew Aunt Tiny's real name. She stood five–foot, two–inches tall and topped three hundred pounds, so I couldn't understand why people called her Tiny. Her nickname was just one more example of that good old Southern kindness I often heard about and seldom saw.

I only recall one visit to Tiny's house. I have a vivid, almost surreal memory of her little dilapidated home, no more than a four-room shack with an outhouse, one with a crescent moon carved into the door. She had a milk cow, chickens, and a little garden with all sorts of good things.

When we arrived, we found her sitting outside in the shade on a circular wooden bench, built around a stout old oak tree. She had her short round legs spread wide under her hiked-up skirt in a not-so-modest attempt to cool herself in the suffocating summer heat. Her legs looked like huge, overstuffed sausages, the rolls of fat mottled with a red heat rash. We sat a while as she snapped peas and shucked corn for our dinner. Later, once it cooled down a bit, I became mesmerized watching her churn butter as she perched precariously spread-legged on the edge of a chair, working a pole up and down in an old wooden barrel.

Aunt Tiny shared my grandmother's obsession with cleanliness. It must have been a part of the Hughey girls' DNA. Aunt Tiny swept her yard every day with a house broom, not a rake. Her yard was as smooth as a floor. Any sticks or rocks you saw were stacked in neat little piles or used to border the flowerbeds or trees.

I didn't like Aunt Tiny much. She seemed to see children the same way she saw yard dogs. I got the clear, yet unspoken message from her to "shut up and stay out from underfoot, and you might get a scrap or two." Eccentricity was a trait found on every twisted branch of our family tree. Some branches were more gnarled than others.

FRED RAYWORTH

Fred Rayworth commenced pursuing this passion in 1995. He's, so far, completed ten full-length novels and is currently working on eleven and twelve, in genres including science fiction, icky bug (horror), adventure/thriller, and fantasy. Multiple short horror stories made it to publication, including "The House", which appeared in the anthology *Between the Pages*, 2003, "The Walk Home" in *Writer's Bloc* 2006, and "The Basement" in *Writer's Bloc II*, 2008. His short science fiction story, "Fun In The Outland," appeared in the anthology *First Voyage* in 2008, while his short fantasy story "Don't Mess With A Snorg" saw publication in the anthology *A World of Their Own* in 2009. His autobiographical short story "Galf" appeared in the anthology *Writer's Bloc IV*, 2012. When not writing, he can be found either making something out of wood in his garage or out under a dark sky pursuing faint fuzzy objects with his telescope.

Dye-No-Myte!

When I was a little kid, I wasn't as innocent as I appeared. In fact, I was quite the mischief maker and daredevil. I almost never got caught, because, "Little Freddie would never do something like that." Those were not my parents' words, but every time someone suspected us kids of something, the neighbors would focus on my friends, who didn't have either the innocent look or the smarts to keep their mouths shut.

I learned early in life the value of silence. In the early '50s, before living in Lompoc (pronounced "lawm-poke," not "lawm-pock"), we lived in Palmdale. I attended part of first grade at Manzanita Elementary. Deathly afraid of the Principal's paddle, though I never experienced it, I'd witnessed plenty of friends that did by giving lip or speaking up when they shouldn't. That kept me on the straight-and-narrow, at least, at school. Whenever I did something, I made sure not to blab or let anyone see me.

At home it was a different story. There was that time my mom found me playing with the little worms in the front yard that turned out to be baby sidewinders, a type of rattlesnake. Once, after watching the TV show Combat!, where the soldiers used flamethrowers, I took an old Black Flag poison sprayer, filled it with gasoline, went out in the middle of our street, and lit the end. My flamethrower caught fire, and I had to throw it down. It ignited the asphalt and burned a big pothole. Not long after that, we moved to Playa del Rey where I made do with sliding down the steep ice plant-covered slopes into the street. Outside

25

of surprising a few cars and coming home with my clothes stained bright green, I did little collateral damage. In all of those cases, an innocent look or silence couldn't help me, because the evidence was irrefutable.

I survived the first grade, and we moved to Lompoc where I continued to take risks. Five years and one police incident later, in the spring of 1963, I was out-and-about with my friends, Roger, Charles, and Bob. On this adventure, we stole keys out of parked cars, because my friend Roger liked to collect them. Back in those days, some cars didn't have them (they had starter buttons), and those that did were often left in the ignition along with house and other keys. Most people didn't lock their doors, either. After emptying every vehicle in the next block over from our neighborhood (not ours, of course), we moved on to a construction yard full of trucks, many with keys.

A truck with unlocked side cabinets caught our eye. I spotted what looked like giant red BB tubes. Back in the day, BB gun ammo came in small red tubes with crimped ends. These giant versions looked the same, except one end didn't slide off. With wide eyes of wonder, I gazed at the label on one which read, High Pressure Gelatin.

"Is it some kind of Jell-O?"

My question got shrugs. One tube twisted open in the middle and it looked like brown sugar with white stuff mixed in. Nobody volunteered to taste it.

We divvied up the sticks. Charles and I ended up with two each and the others one. Bob got the one that twisted open.

"We'd better get out of here before someone sees us," Charles said.

With a bulging bag of keys, plus our new-found treasure, we headed to the underground drainage pipe on College Avenue, across the street from the construction yard.

The drainpipe provided an excellent play haven. It ran for several blocks and a railroad track lay parallel to it. Deep inside the tunnel, trains rumbled by, almost overhead. This provided endless thrills!

We climbed down into the entrance culvert and examined our prizes in more detail.

"This stuff doesn't look like Jell-O to me." Bob peered into the gap in his twisted open stick.

"They are kind of shaped like giant firecrackers," I suggested.

"Maybe, it's flammable." Charles grabbed an old spoon lying in a nearby pile of trash.

I grabbed it from him and bent over Bob's open stick, which he'd put on the ground. I dug a chunk out and dabbed it on the cement. "How we goin' to light it?"

"Try this." Roger gave me some matches.

I struck one and touched it to the stuff. It wouldn't light. I tried several more to no avail.

"Here." Charles knelt down and poured on some rubbing alcohol he'd also found in the truck. When I touched it with another lit match, the alcohol flared up, but the brown sugar stuff still didn't do anything for a moment. All of a sudden, it erupted like a highway flare.

"Cool!" everyone said at once.

Roger waved his around. "We should keep these flares and figure a way to light them for the Fourth of July."

The dab of gelatin burned out. Roger had his bag of keys. It was dinner time, so we headed home. My pair of sticks went in the overgrown brush in the alley behind my house.

A few months passed, the sticks all but forgotten. Then one Saturday morning, I sat home alone, watching Deputy Dawg cartoons on TV. My sister was at a friend's house and my dad worked overtime at Point Arguello while my mom did her usual weekend appointments at her beauty shop. A knock at the door interrupted my fun. To my surprise, it was The Heat, The Fuzz, a pair of Coppers!

In my mind, I ran through all the things I could've done to send out the cops. Charles and I had caught fire to that field two months before. There were the stink seeds I crushed in class. Then I spotted Roger standing behind them, looking worried. What had Roger and I done?

"Hello, son. Would you please tell us where you hid the dynamite?"

Say what? "Uh, Sir, I don't have any dynamite."

Behind our faithful public servants, Roger waved frantically and mouthed, "The flares!"

"Please tell us where you put the dynamite."

He didn't even ask if my mom or dad were home. In retrospect, I think our fine officers were a bit upset.

I've been known to be rather dense, but, suddenly, Roger's pantomime hit home. "You mean the flares?"

"Son, they're not flares."

Oh crap!

"Where are they?"

So much for Deputy Dawg.

"Please, go to the side gate. I have to put my dog in the house." I pointed to the left.

I went to the kitchen door and let Fritzi, our long-haired weenie dawg inside. Then I led the three of them through the back yard and into the alley. By this time, I had to look for the flares, because the weeds had grown. Luckily for everyone, my dad hadn't made me mow it all down. I probably would've forgotten the sticks were there. I finally found them and pushed back the weeds so they could be seen.

"Holy crap, get back from there!"

"Say what?" I looked up to see the older cop with a wild look in his eyes and his hand on his holster. My hand was about an inch above one of the large red sticks.

The younger cop stood next to his partner and gazed down at the sticks. "Those things are huge."

"Son, very carefully, step back."

The two cops talked to each other as if we weren't there.

"They didn't tell us they were that big," the young one said.

"I got this. You go take care of the other contacts and come back for me." This old guy had a bit of a shake to his hands. The other one left.

"My name's Homer." He took a seat across the alley in the neighbor's trash can recess (a hole in their fence to hold trash cans). "Sorry to get so upset, but I need to tell you why those things are so dangerous. Why any explosives are so dangerous. Conventional explosives, when they age, develop nitrogen whiskers. That's a chemical process that affects not only dynamite, but also bullets, like I have in my belt." He pointed to his waist. "All policemen are required to keep their ammo clean to prevent these nitrogen whiskers. The whiskers are crystallized chemicals from the explosives inside each bullet. Just the slightest touch, a breeze, a radio signal can set them off. With your two sticks being exposed to the outside for several months, they're prime candidates to go boom!"

Roger and I looked at each other.

"We never saw the stick they recovered at your friend's house." Homer jerked his thumb toward the west.

In my naiveté, I had no idea he was talking about Roger, whose house was toward the west.

The old cop gazed at the explosives lying in the weeds. "I didn't know they were so huge. They just said these were big ones."

They still looked like giant BB packages to me...well, flares. Dynamite sticks always seemed skinnier, at least, from what I saw on TV.

"We have to call a team from Vandenberg Air Force Base, because we have no bomb squad here in town. They're called EOD, which stands for Explosive Ordinance Disposal. They're the nearest experts that can safely recover these things." Homer then gave me the look.

Those eyes made me feel very guilty. Why, I didn't know, but something about the authority and the badge got to me. I couldn't help but go back to my old habits of keeping my mouth shut. Silence helped me avoid lots of trouble. However, with the evidence lying on the ground right next to me, it would be hard to pull the "innocent little Freddie" game.

"Okay, son, do you know where the rest of the dynamite is?"

Keep your mouth shut. Don't be a ratfink. I shook my head.
"Are you sure?"

Roger kept giving me facial and hand signals, which I assumed meant not to tell the cops anything. I didn't know he'd already told them I might know who had the other sticks, and where. Why he didn't remember, I never found out.

"Please. A lot of people might get hurt or killed."

Those eyes. Don't tell.

It wasn't about anyone getting hurt. It was all about being a ratfink. At first.

"Son, I don't know much about dynamite, but from the size of those sticks, one of those going off could probably level your house and the one behind it. Two going off..." He glanced up and down the alley.

That gave me pause. People getting hurt? Don't rat on your friends. Hell with it.

"I know where the other sticks are." At least, I didn't give him any names.

The old cop gave an exasperated sigh. "If you need to make some calls, go do it now."

I walked back inside, feeling a mix of ratfink and relief. So much for silent, innocent little Freddie. When I opened the kitchen door, Fritzi squeezed by and ran toward the back gate. I ran after him, but he barreled into the alley. He went straight to the two sticks and peed on them.

Old Homer about had a stroke. He forgot where he was, jumped up in that trash recess and almost knocked himself out. I ran over, grabbed Fritzi, and went inside, all the while trying not to let Homer see me laughing.

I called Charles, two doors down. "Those flares we found—"

"Hey, what're the cops doing at your house?"

"I'm trying to tell you. Remember those flares? Where did you put yours?" I knew exactly where they were.

"What about them?"

"That's why the cops are here. They're dynamite!"

The other end fell silent. I was about to speak when Charles finally replied. "Did you tell them my name?"

"We have to. They could blow up your house! These guys from Vandenberg have to come get them. You don't have time to take them somewhere else."

"I have to, at least, throw them under my brother's bed. They'll find my Playboys."

We hung up just as this official Air Force truck pulled out in front of my house. I ran back to tell Homer and rat out one of my best friends.

With the bomb squad there to collect my dynamite and invade Charles' place, Homer put Roger, Charles, and me in the back seat of the squad car and off we went with his partner to find the final one. Unfortunately, with two cops in the car, we couldn't communicate freely. My lousy skill at charades became worse when Roger tried to tell me what not to say.

I'd already opened my big mouth about Bob's dynamite. We went on a wild goose chase all over Lompoc as I led the cops from one fake location to another. I could tell they were getting pretty pissed off. After the fifth stop, the three of us found some alone time, probably engineered by the cops in a last-ditch effort to get me to tell the truth.

Roger grabbed my shirt. "What're you doing? I thought you knew where the other stick was!"

"I thought you didn't want me to get Bob in trouble." I gave Charles a glance, but he seemed to be enjoying it all.

"You can show them where the stick is without telling them his name. I just don't want you to mention his name."

Duh. I glanced over at the cops who stood in a huddle facing away from us. "How did you get caught?"

Roger's face turned red. "I had mine in the garage. I didn't like having it around. It made me nervous, so I threw it away in the neighbor's trash. The crabapple saw me. He about wet his pants when he saw what it was. He called the cops right away. Next thing I know, my place was swarming with them."

"So, you ratfinked on me." I didn't feel so bad, now.

"I didn't have a choice. What did you expect? I don't want to see anyone dead."

"You didn't tell your old man what we were doing when we found them, did you?" Charles asked.

"Of course not." Roger spat on the ground. "I just said we were out messing around and found that truck."

Homer came back over. "Okay, have you guys decided to tell us the real story?"

I ended up having to tell them Bob's name, anyway, because I wasn't exactly sure where he threw the stick. Once again, I broke my rule of silence, became a ratfink, but all for a good cause. I took them to Tha' Ditch, a very deep V-shaped canal that ran from the town's flood control basin to the Santa Inez river. It also happened to run along V Street, so its shape fit the street name perfectly.

The look on Bob's face was priceless when we showed up at the door with a pair of cops, but we didn't have time to rib him about it. After a brief explanation, he led the cops across the street and was about to go to the spot in Tha' Ditch when EOD showed up. They'd already finished up at Charles' and my house. When Bob led the Air Force guy down the slope to where he'd tossed his twisted open treasure, it had lain all those months fully exposed to the elements.

"Get back, son!"

Bob scrambled back up the slope, his eyes wide.

The Air Force guy came up right behind him. He got on the radio and called his bosses. "I'm still here in Lawm-pock—"

The four of us, two of the cops and, at least, one of the Air Force guys all turned to him and said, "It's Lawm-Poke!"

The Airman stopped speaking, looked at everyone with his mouth open, corrected his pronunciation, listened a moment, and then ordered the cops to evacuate the neighborhood, something we later learned they didn't have to do back at my house or Charles'. They merely picked them up after confirming they were stable. We received our second, much quicker lecture on nitrogen whiskers while he grabbed his gear from the back of their truck.

The cops whisked us all to headquarters, and we got "the talk." That was the second time Charles and I had been there since the window-breaking incident many years earlier. The next day, we became anonymous celebrities. The Lompoc Record, our local newspaper, had an article called Those Lucky Boys (names withheld because of our ages, of course). I used to have a copy of that article in a scrapbook, but the scrapbook has gone missing. Someday, I'll contact the paper to get a copy.

In the aftermath, we never found out what those huge sticks of dynamite were used for or what they were doing in that truck. Even worse, nobody reported them missing. We did learn that Homer was either exaggerating about their blast radius or simply didn't know. Also, the part about cleaning his bullets was not true. Then again, because of the size of the sticks and with Charles and I having four of them in such close proximity, if they'd all gone off at the same time, as unlikely as it was, the shock wave could've flattened several houses.

All it would've taken was for one nitrogen whisker to break the wrong way and you never would've heard this story. Not from me, anyway. Dye-No-Myte!

FICTION

SYDNEE ELLIOT

Sydnee Elliot, writer and painter, is originally from Chelsea, Massachusetts and attended Boston University. After graduation and one failed marriage, she moved to Berkeley. Ten years later she moved to Las Vegas and worked in the gambling industry for twenty years. While in Las Vegas, she studied playwriting at UNLV. In 1995, Sydnee moved to Greece, her life-long dream finally achieved. During her ten-year stay on the island of Kythera, she wrote short stories and completed one novel, *Polly's Wild Dance: A Life Serialized in Sporadic Spurts.*

Polly's Wild Dance and *Lost and Found*, a collection of short stories, are available on Amazon. Sydnee lives in Las Vegas, Nevada and is editing her second novel, *Polly's World*, the prequel to *Polly's Wild Dance* and *Get What You Deserve*, a cheeky, humorous murder mystery.

Obituary

"DON'T WANT OLD BURNT TOAST. Don't want that tepid green water you call tea," Jennie shouted as Nurse Carol entered the room carrying her breakfast tray. Nurse Carol, always steady on her feet, staggered at the unusual tone of Jennie's voice, nearly colliding with the flowery chintz chair by the door. Ordinarily, Jennie Block never spoke above a whisper, a habit left over from her librarian days.

"I don't want my apple mid-morning either. Stay away, stay away, I'll be busy all day."

Jennie stooped over her unmade bed, separating small pieces of paper into different piles.

Frazzled, Nurse Carol returned to the nurses' station. "Room 12 is acting out of sorts." The other nurses ignored her. Room 15 had soiled the bed three times within the last two hours. They were discussing cutting Room 15 off, no food or drink, at least, not until he was back to normal.

At noon, Nurse Carol headed for Jennie's room.

"Hey, Jennie. Time for lunch. Macaroni and cheese, piping hot, just the way you like it."

"Don't want lunch." Jennie's voice reverberated down the hall. "Hold the orange at snack time. Got a lot to sort out today; don't want any distractions."

Nurse Carol's head bobbed about like a chicken in heat. Meals were important to Jennie, the timing of them signified which part of the day had been subtracted and which portion remained.

Today was Jennie's fifth-year anniversary in the Stay

37

Well Nursing Home. She voluntarily moved to the nursing home after she mistook the old lampshade splattered with antelope heads for the wood stove in the kitchen and almost burned the house down. The staff considered her a model member of the geriatric community; her demands were minimal.

Jennie received copies of newspapers from the surrounding towns of Cherryville, Plattersville, Centerville, and Honesty every morning. It wasn't the news she sought. What interested her most were the obituaries of people she'd never met. She read each obit in detail, then snipped out the most exciting ones with her small pointy cuticle trimmers. After clipping them together with black bobby pins, she placed them in a manila folder labeled "Unique Dead People." She kept the folder in the drawer of the table next to her bed and reread the clippings often. She'd count them, gently tap them, then emphatically declare the most recent total, "One hundred and fifty-two to date."

"Are you sick, Jennie?" Nurse Carol asked after she refused lunch. "We depend on you to stay well, you know. We count on you being our model patient. You never give us any trouble at all." The nurse squinted and scrutinized the mess on Jennie's usually tidy bed.

Jennie's Unique Dead People's folder was open. Piles of obituaries were spread over the coverlet. She scribbled on the yellow-lined pad she kept on her nightstand.

"What are you doing, Jennie?"

"Don't ever call me Jennie again. My name's Arora, without the 'u'."

"Okay, Arora. But why Arora?"

"Has a nicer ring to it than Jennie; no special ring to Jennie. Besides, it's a fun word; spelled the same backward and forward. That's called a palindrome. Can't make palindromes out of all words, yet all words can be turned around any way. Sometimes, a word spelled backward sounds a lot nicer than it does forward. Gives one a different perspective on things."

"What are you doing with all these obituaries?"

"Statistics."

"Want some help?"

"No, thanks, Lorac, I can manage on my own. There's a song in Lorac." Jennie smiled at the nurse. "Can you hear it?"

"Who's Lorac? What are you talking about?"

Nurse Carol's brow furrowed. The nurses had their hands full with those recognizably fogged in; they didn't need another one jumping off the deep end.

"You're Lorac. Like it? Has a nice ring, doesn't it?" Jennie's eyes sparkled like splinters of purple and green glass as the sun twinkled through the window, illuminating her melon-shaped face.

"I guess so, if you say so, Jen . . . Arora."

Hastily, Nurse Carol returned to her station with the bad news.

"Well, gals, Room 12's gone ditzy. Her name's Arora now, without the u. And I'm Lorac."

Nurse Jane, head honcho, slammed her plump authoritative hand on the desk. She wobbled out from behind it leaving her half-eaten peanut butter and banana sandwich oozing on a paper plate. She hooked her thumbs through the thick uniform fabric into the waistband of her pantyhose and hitched them upward like John Wayne shifting his holster.

"I'll go take a look-see. I can communicate with the worst of them."

With an exasperated huff, she marched toward Room 12, arms swinging and toting her humongous backside like a caboose pulling a dilapidated freight train.

"Hey, Jennie, how're we today? Heard we're having a problem. Want to talk about it?"

Nurse Jane pulled the blanket from side to side in a militant attempt to make the bed. Jennie gripped her pad of paper like a medical clipboard. She flashed Nurse Jane a deadly glance before placing her pad on the nightstand. Jennie jumped at the nurse with closed fists, punching her pudgy arms as if they were cymbals in the Fourth of July parade.

"You leave my things alone. You're disrupting my system. In case you haven't heard, I'm Arora, without the u. Until the day I die, I'm Arora. Nice ring to it, huh? Spelled the same backward and forward. Now, please, Enaj, leave me be. Can't you see how busy I am?"

"What's an Enaj?"

"You are. Nice ring to it, don't you think? Tell Nurse Lorac not to bring me food till I ask. I've got a busy day ahead of me." Jennie continued with her statistics.

Nurse Jane strutted back to the station. She squished her peanut butter and banana sandwich flat against the plate with her fist into a narrow, paper-thin square. Soft gooshy banana shot out from between the bleached slices of bread and landed on the desk. She folded the square into quarters and plopped it into her mouth swallowing it whole. A waste-not, want-not type, she scooped the dribbles of banana up with her index finger and licked it clean. With her last lick, her eyes rolled upward. Dr. Goodfellow's strict order posted on the bulletin board caught her attention:

IF A PATIENT REFUSES TO EAT, CALL ME IMMEDIATELY!

Any Time of Day or Night!
Dr. Christopher Goodfellow

Death follows loss of appetite and depression. Disruption of government sustenance payments due to a patient's death puts the well-being of the Stay Well Nursing Home and its employees in jeopardy. "No money, no honey," he shouted at his staff during meetings.

Nurse Jane frantically dialed the doctor's private number.

"Hello, Dr. Goodfellow. Nurse Jane here. Problem. Room 12 refuses food. She's talking nonsense."

Jennie was standing by the window when the doctor arrived, her cheeks flushed with excitement. Thin alabaster strands of hair cascaded around her face. A waning bun precariously sat a bit off center from where it customarily perched on top of her head. She looked like an antique kewpie doll someone had scavenged from the bottom of an old trunk.

"Jennie, my favorite young lady, how are we today?"

"Ah, Dr. Wollefdoog, exactly the person I want to see. How do you like your new name? Nice ring to it, huh? Sounds like something one might hear coming from a person who just surprised himself by jumping off a cliff. Since you're the one in charge, here are the instructions to be followed after I die."

"Well, Jennie, I'm not going to let you leave us so easily. You're going to be with us for a long, long time. After all, we're one big family here."

Jennie smiled. Family, ha! Haven't had one for years; certainly don't need one now, you big puffed up ball of steaming smelly farts. Who gave you the last say about who will die and who won't and when and where?

From the age of seven until now, at ninety-three, Jennie followed a simple path, one without bumps or curves. Her decisions depended upon supply and demand. In 1926, when the library needed a librarian, she needed a job, and certification for such a position in Cherryville didn't exist.

Jennie patted the doctor's arm. Imagine leaving this idiot in charge of writing my obituary. Who knows what he'd put into the newspaper if left on his own.

"Dr. Wollefdoog, from now on, please call me Arora, without the 'u'. You see these bits and pieces? Well, all these people are dead." She pointed to the display of death notices laid out on her faded green blanket. "These obituaries reveal their thoughts about the most important happenings in their lives and all the things they loved to do."

Jennie wasn't concerned with what these people had done, but what she hadn't done. The need to rectify this had become a source of concern and energy for her ever since she extracted her first obituary from the Cherryville News several years ago. She saved the ones with spicy, stirring names, along with those describing lovely pastimes. Lives lived with passion and verve interested her the most. A mirror image of her own dispassionate life taunted her with possibilities. But she was still alive; she still had hope.

"Jennie, Arora, stop this nonsense. Eat some lunch. Your blood sugar level probably dropped. You're hallucinating." The doctor checked his watch.

"Look, here." She shoved her yellow pad of paper with all its checkmarks under the good doctor's nose. "Out of one hundred and fifty-two lives, thirty-seven women loved to knit and crochet, twenty-five loved to quilt and grow roses, seven loved to fish, twelve loved to play cards, five loved cats, while only two loved dogs. Here, look." She pushed her sliding bun on top of her head only to have it slip down on the other side. "Remember, the key word is 'loved.' Three men and two women loved doing jigsaw puzzles. One man had a special love for his grandchildren. Another believed strongly in 'Cleanliness is next to Godliness.' He claimed to have used the same knife his granddaddy had given him back in 1893 when he was a lad to clean his ears and fingernails with, which he continued to do until the day he died at 102.

"Here are a few more interesting women. One had a passion for tying the wings of flies into knots. I wondered about this one and how she managed to hold on to the tiny things long enough to knot their wings. It doesn't matter, she loved doing it. Some of them did daring, interesting things like this woman who took herself to a nunnery, then became consumptive. She was forced to return to a life she didn't want in the first place. What bravery!

"Eight women loved to laugh, play bingo, and socialize. I can see how these three things go well together. Ha, only four had a passion for watching television, and it says they will miss doing that, now that they've moved on to the hereafter. Tells something about their generation, doesn't it? They understood the importance of things, and it wasn't the television."

"Arora, I'm leaving, I—"

"Wait, it gets better."

Dr. Goodfellow pointed at his watch. "It's five-forty-five. I'm meeting my wife at six-thirty for dinner. Jen...Arora, you're upsetting my schedule. You must eat something. You'll get sick and die if you don't."

"That's exactly what this is all about. Here's my obituary. I don't want a word of it changed. I'm beginning to work on the truth of what I've written. My plan is to enhance every aspect of my life until the day I pass on. I didn't live an interesting life. The importance of passion eluded me. There isn't much that can be said about me to make a good read. So I've decided to change as much of this as is in my power. I've enjoyed reading the interesting parts of people's lives and want to leave something exciting for readers and collectors of obituaries after I pass on. No one's left to know whether my stories are true or not, so I've decided to enhance what little I have, beginning with the plain name I've lived with all my life. I've changed my name to Arora Barmecide. Or, better yet, Arora Edicemrab. Sounds like the name of a beautiful vegetable. I'm not crazy about vegetables, but I'd eat one with a name like that." Jennie's voice reached an almost perfect soprano pitch.

She shook a handful of obits in front of Dr. Goodfellow's face. "This one's called Homily. Here, look. Letrina and Velvet. Yes. Velvet like the soft, pulpy fabric, and Ulli and Florinda. Now there's a melody for you. What about this one, Faustos? I would've hitched my wagon to a man with such a name. What about Lysander? I read about a Lysander once. Lysander Spooner, self-proclaimed individualist and anarchist. We need someone like him today to be president. No chance for someone with a name like Lysander to fail in life." Arora gathered her clippings and placed them in their folders. "Now read this."

Dr. Goodfellow grabbed the piece of paper Arora held out to him. The roadmap of veins on the back of her steady, chalky white hand relaxed once she was relieved of its burden.

He read slowly, whispering the words. Arora listened as the doctor read, nodding her approval.

ARORA BARMECIDE ALSO KNOWN AS ARORA EDICEMRAB, BORN ON ZZYZX ROAD IN THE LOVELY TOWN OF PAHRUMP. SHE LIVED OUT HER LIFE IN CHERRYVILLE AS A LIBRARIAN AND SPENT HER REMAINING DAYS RECITING PROPER CHRISTIAN NAMES AND NOUNS IN REVERSE. SHE RECITED AND SPELLED THE NAMES OF ALL THE CAPITAL CITIES IN AMERICA, INVERTED, WITHIN THREE MINUTES' TIME. SHE PRIDED HERSELF ON THIS ABILITY BECAUSE SHE LOVED HER COUNTRY, AND, ABOVE ALL ELSE, LOVED WITH GRANDIOSE PASSION, THE MUSICAL SOUNDS OF INVERTED PROPER NAMES AND ALL OTHER COMMON THINGS.

"You can add only, and I mean only, the essential details later, like date of birth, date of death, and cause of death. Nothing more, nothing less. Forget about my proper family. Family and friends have all been dead for years."

"Listen, Jennie...Arora, I don't know about this. You've lived right here in Cherryville all your life. Besides, I've never heard of such a road or town. People around here will know it's a lie." Dr. Goodfellow wiped the sweat from his brow with a crumpled Kleenex.

"Cherryville. No ring to it. Too fruity. No zip. I'm looking for zip. Take, for example, Zzyzx and Pahrump, or Xzyzz and Pmurhap. Listen to the melody, the cadence, the almost aria of it all. These are real places, only not close to each other. Geographically." Jennie slammed the drawer shut. Her dead people folder tucked away safely, she took a stance, feet apart, eye-to-eye with the only person left to carry out her wishes after she was gone. "Do you mean to tell me someone will actually try to find these places on a map only to contradict me? So what if some of it's a lie. All of life's a lie. What won't be a lie is I'll already be dead. And I'll have dead the way I want it. For those who try to contradict my facts, tell 'em to go suck on a frog's fluttering lip. Didn't you once mention, in passing, you're originally from Notsob, and went to school in Aihpledalihp? Practiced that one all morning. Nice ring to it, don't you think?"

"What's this Barmecide?" I'll humor her. Get her to eat. Then I'm off. What a whacko. Names, changes, reversals, and life endings. Bah.

"Always favored the word Barmecide. Sounds like some sort of soft drink, medicinal, good for the stomach. It means illusion, giving way to disappointment, like the story of the prince serving a beggar a feast consisting of ornate but empty dishes. Guess life is what we make it. Now, where's my dinner? I'm starved. Today I want some of the ugly looking thing they cook back there, the big green bushy stuff that looks like a chopped down tree and smells bad. I need my strength."

"Broccoli?" He raised his eyebrows. Five residents died in the last six months. "No money, no honey," he recited in his head. Jennie's on a roll. She'll eat and not die and the monthly payments will continue. He smiled.

"Iloccorb, guess so, nice ring to it, huh? Maybe I'll expand my list to include other vegetables; maybe, some new fruits. Never concerned myself much with anything except saep. Like the tiny, round neatness of them, so self-contained. Same with selppa and segnaro. No surprises there except if they're rotten inside."

"I'll let Nurse Jane know you plan on changing your diet." He raced down the hall.

"Doctor, is she crazy?" Nurse Jane licked chocolate off her palm. "Old ones like her, they flip fast."

"Hardly. Feed her anything she wants." He laughed. "Get her some iloccorb for lunch," he said and streaked out the door.

Jennie swung around in circles; arms splayed child-like trying to hug the moon. Her white flannel granny nightgown morphed into a haunted wedding gown mushrooming, rippling, and dancing to the sound of its own private waltz.

HOWIE ERICKSON

Howie Erickson graduated from the University of Saskatchewan with a Masters Degree in Computer Automation. He worked in Canada, the United States, Malaysia, Borneo, and Yemen. He currently lives in Calgary, Alberta, with his wife Lorraine and their dog, Sophie.

He has been actively involved in the Calgary writing community for a number of years and recently served on the board of the Alexandra Writer's' Centre Society, a society that provides training and support for Calgary writers. His short story "Intentions" was published in the fall 2013 issue of *OnSpec Magazine*. His first novel *The Bloodline Artifacts* will be published in 2014.

A Sunny Day in Boston

Joel Simpson started to relax as he walked through Boston's Christopher Columbus Waterfront Park. He'd spent the morning in his office going over and over the calculations. He could find nothing wrong, but when the President of the United States was involved, well, you couldn't be too careful.

This was his favorite noon-hour walk. He'd take the MTA Blue Line to the Aquarium Station then walk through the park, under the wisteria-covered trellis, and out onto Long Wharf. Today, the weather was perfect, the wisteria was in full bloom, there was no wind, and the sun was warm on his face.

An arm reached from behind and tightened around his neck. A finger stuck into his back. "Gi'me that lunch bag there or it's your life," a voice whispered.

"How do you know it's lunch and not say, dead squirrels?" Joel said, as he tried to squirm out of the grip of his assailant.

"Because it's your turn to bring lunch and you don't like squirrel," Rodney Smitt said, as he fell into step beside Joel.

"You know, Rodney, one of these times there's going to be a cop nearby, and he'll think you're up to no good."

"Me, in an Armani suit? He wouldn't dare."

They continued out on the wharf, picked a table looking out at the ocean, and Joel produced two corned beef sandwiches, a root beer, and a coke. "Here you go, one squirrel sandwich and a root beer."

Rodney smiled. "So, how's the project going, today's the big day, isn't it? The test firing, right?"

Joel took a bite of his sandwich.

"Well, today's the day, right. And the President, he's still involved?" Rodney said. "I haven't seen anything on the news about the President for a few days. Is it your Bull's-eye Project? Is that where he is?"

Joel leaned forward and whispered, "Shit, Rodney. It's top secret. And there are ears here." He tilted his head toward a nearby table where a couple had quit talking and were obviously doing a little eavesdropping. "I'll fill you in later."

The crew snapped to attention as President Zagon stepped onto the flight deck with the captain of the Galaxy Explorer. The President made the rounds with the captain, smiling and shaking hands with various crew members as they made their way past a bank of computers to a small dais that had been set up for the President.

"Ladies and Gentlemen, scientists and crew of the Galaxy Explorer, I am proud to be here with you today. I believe that this test is so momentous that I have taken several days away from my regular duties. If successful, we will have developed a weapon of such deterrent power that it could prevent future inter-stellar wars and the needless death of millions, perhaps billions of people. We could well go down in history as the group that ensured the survival of our species."

President Zagon waited for a polite round of applause to die down.

"Captain, are we ready?"

"Yes, President Zagon, Sir."

"Then let's proceed."

The Captain escorted the president to a small console. "President Zagon, Sir, sit right here. You will fire the device by pushing this button." The captain lifted a protective white cover to reveal a blue button.

"And what will happen then?" the President said.

"Ah...President Zagon, Sir, perhaps, the project leader could explain it better than I can?"

The President nodded and the Captain motioned to a woman in light green coveralls.

"President Zagon, Sir, this is Amorpha, the project leader. She can explain the weapon's operation. "

"President Zagon, Sir, the project team has developed what could be called a quantum canon. In quantum physics, a particle can be in two places at once," Amorpha said.

"I've been told that before, but it seems a little hard to believe. How is that possible?"

"President Zagon, Sir, nobody is quite sure. Lots of mathematical proofs and quite a number of experiments seem to validate the theory, but really, no one knows for sure how it works. The scientists do the calculations, and we build the device and test it. If it works, we all pat ourselves on the back; if it doesn't, the scientists revise their theories."

"This is the first real test of this device?"

Amorpha nodded. "President Zagon, Sir, that is correct."

"Is there any danger to us or our planet?"

"President Zagon, Sir, there is no danger. We have done enough testing to ensure that we are safe, and we are out beyond the asteroid belt, firing away from our sun, so our world will be safe."

"Okay, so this quantum canon, what does it do?" The president said.

"President Zagon, Sir, we fire a quantum particle. One particle is here in our time-space, the other is near the actual target. In the process, the mass of our particle is reduced and the energy of the other increases. If we could take that process to completion, we could completely convert the mass of our particle to energy in the other location. That would give us a weapon of almost unimaginable power."

"But, we can't completely convert the mass to energy?" the president said.

"President Zagon, Sir, you are correct, but none-the-less, the weapon should be very powerful, powerful enough to destroy a star."

The Captain stepped forward. "President, Sir, we are ready to test the weapon. You may proceed when you wish."

"Yes, I'm ready. I just lift the white cover and push the blue button, correct?"

"Yes, President Zagon, Sir. You may want to adjust the three lenses on the quantum viewer to fit your eyes before you push the button. The viewer will allow you to see the results of the test."

The President adjusted each of the three lenses on the viewer. "So, it's that small star that we are targeting? Are we sure the system has no sentient life?"

"President Zagon, Sir, we are. We have been beaming quantum signals at the system for some time now without response. There certainly is no sentient life in that system."

The President lifted the white safety cover and put his finger on the blue button. "A small push by one ensures the survival of all." He pushed the button and the ship shuttered. Everyone held their breath.

Rodney swallowed the last bite of his sandwich and washed it down with a swig of root beer as the couple at the nearby table stood and wandered off. "Okay, Joel, no one is listening now. What's up?"

"We're doing the test today. No one knows for sure if it will work. I did all the calculations. It's my baby, so if it fails...well..." Joel said.

"So, why aren't you there?" Rodney asked.

"I don't know. I should be, but for security reasons they just sent the project leader. She doesn't understand the math but can handle the brass."

"I was right then. That's why the President's been out of the news for the last couple of weeks, right?"

Joel shrugged.

"And they're testing, what did you call it, a quantum weapon? In Nevada, Project Bull's-eye, right?"

"Shit, Rodney, I shouldn't have told you any of this. You're such a blabber-mouth."

"Ah, come on. Am I right?"

"Well, it is a quantum weapon and the President is going to fire it, but the test is not in Nevada, it's in…shit, holy shit. Look," Joel said as he pointed up.

A long streak of plasma streamed out of one side of the sun. The opposite side flattened and then—the sun exploded.

President Zagon pulled his head back from the trinocular quantum viewer, slammed his fist on the desk, and let out a roar of laughter. "Well, we sure centre-eyed that little star."

Some of the crew and scientists chuckled, but most appeared uncertain, should they laugh or not? They were all aware that, in a rage, prior to his appointment, the Vice President, who was much shorter than the President, had climbed up on a chair and punched the President in his center eye, knocking President Zagon off his feet. The media had coined the term, "center-eyed," for a knockout punch.

President Zagon wandered about, laughing, shaking hands, trying to charm smiles from the crew and scientists with comments about center-eying the little star.

RICHARD J. FELLER

Richard Feller is a graduate of California State University, Fullerton with a B.A. in Marketing. He has been a member of the Henderson Writers' Group of Nevada for three years. His passion for writing provides a welcomed escape from the stress of everyday life. He particularly enjoys writing short story fiction with dark undercurrents of human drama. One day he hopes to fulfill a dream of finding a home for his unpublished novel and labor of love, *A Certain Smile*. You can contact Rick at rickfeller@aol.com.

Sign of Life

Aubrey lay semiconscious beneath the blanket on her hospital bed. Though thirty-eight, her body ached with the frailties of a woman decades older. Her blistered skin hung over her bones like an oversized shirt. Beneath her hair of brittle gray threads, a face carved with deep lines. Like rings of a tree, each conveyed the hard life that had left her broken, bruised, and disfigured from years of abuse.

Too weak to breathe on her own, the rhythmic gasps of the ventilator cried out for an end to this journey in her desperate desire for peace. After years of drugs and numerous attempts at court-ordered rehab, she recognized herself as just another statistic, another addict clinging to a few tattered strands of a worthless life.

Aubrey struggled to open her eyes, but she found little more than the murkiness of a lonely room. Visitors appeared only long enough to sign the chart that logged the minutes until the next empty bed. She blamed no one else for her situation. Hers was the result of a lifetime of poor choices. The good memories that remained were fragments of her years in school, a time when innocence brought life to her soul.

Once popular in high school, she'd made cheerleader captain her senior year. Back then, she had long thick golden hair and soft smooth skin. Though desired by the boys, her heart remained with her best friend since elementary school. She could almost feel her heart beat, that summer of her sixteenth birthday, when James finally asked her out on a real date.

But today, beneath a heavy hospital blanket, she passed in and out of consciousness. She grimaced when she felt the painful sting of someone tugging at the tubes and wires that extended from her arms. All at once, a lighter than air calm enveloped her body and carried her away. The tunnel, through which she traveled, pulsated with bright swirling white light. Her mind soon emptied and peace accepted her in a warm embrace.

Aubrey closed her eyes and listened to the melodic hum of distant music. She prayed, as she did every day, to be forgiven for ending the life of the one she loved. Abruptly, the melody transformed into a loud unnerving shriek of chaotic sound.

Aubrey's eyes popped open to find herself seated in her father's dreary brown Ranger truck. He drove along the deserted country road near their home, passing rows of pine trees that fronted the burning orange and red hues of sunset. It was a beautiful sight from her childhood, long forgotten.

Her high school friend Dylan sat beside her, dressed in a black suit. He looked every bit the gentleman she remembered. He'd combed his light brown hair straight back, held down with a generous amount of mousse. Though, he was sprinkled with, perhaps, too much cologne.

Her dad pulled in front of the high school into a commotion of cars and people. After he stopped alongside the curb, she delighted at the sight of the familiar banner above the entrance to the auditorium, Welcome to Prom Night.

Her memories remained foggy on the details of that evening. Aubrey wondered if this was death, a final glimpse of her once blossoming future before it withered away. When she sensed her mind slipping, she surrendered. Aubrey drifted deeper into the thoughts and emotions of the person that embodied her past.

Dylan held her hand as she stepped from the truck and then caught her when one of her heels angled off a small stone. She regained her balance and examined her strapless turquoise gown. Fortunately, she saw no rips or missing sequins.

Her father leaned in before Dylan could shut the truck door. He spoke in a stern tone. "I expect you both out here by midnight…don't be late. AND YOU." He leered at Dylan. "No funny stuff."

He flinched before responding with his usual politeness. "Don't worry, Mr. Adams. I'll take good care of Aubrey. You can trust me."

"Okay then." Her father nodded. "Enjoy yourselves."

Dylan shut the door and the truck drove off.

Aubrey had dated Dylan for almost a month. She'd been aware of his eyeing her during class and after school cheerleader practices for the last couple semesters. She figured he'd be a safe date until her boyfriend James crawled back and begged for forgiveness. Aubrey wasn't even sure if the rumor she'd heard about James was true. But it didn't matter. Real or not, the embarrassment damaged her reputation in the eyes of her friends and fellow classmates.

Dylan squeezed Aubrey's hand and escorted her inside the auditorium. The decorations were colorful and fun, in keeping with the psychedelic '60s theme. The DJ spun music that mixed period songs with those more current. Moving to the beat, most everyone crowded on and around the dance floor.

While dancing with Dylan, she noticed James laughing with his circle of friends, yet he peppered her with sad-eyed glances. Even though he brought no date, she had not planned to speak with him or create a scene. A star on the football team, James stood over six feet. He was gorgeous and blessed with the lush dark hair she longed to run her fingers through.

Later, when Dylan excused himself to use the restroom, Aubrey decided to join her friends. But her thoughts lingered hard on James, and like a magnet, pulled her in his direction.

Their eyes locked. Without a word, his friends became quiet and stepped aside.

"What are you looking at?" she exploded, resisting the desire to kiss and take him back.

James shrugged. "It hurts to see you with him. I miss you."

Aubrey pulled away when he reached for her hand. "I'm here with Dylan. You should've thought of that before sticking your tongue down Sharon's throat."

"Aubrey, it's not what you think. My friends dared me to kiss her to prove I wasn't whipped. It was stupid. I just wanna a second chance."

He now confirmed kissing that slut Sharon at the mall. "There are no second chances. Now, I'm with someone who appreciates me." Though angry that he'd ruined her prom, she knew in her heart that they were destined to be together. She'd already decided to forgive him after a couple more days of punishment.

Aubrey whirled her golden locks behind her and stomped off, not allowing James to say another word. While she lumbered around the dance floor, her thoughts dwelt on the uncomfortable familiarity in their argument. She felt woozy and braced herself against the snack table until the sensation subsided.

After finishing a cup of punch, Aubrey asked a friend if she'd seen Dylan. Following her friend's directions, she pushed through the backdoor exit into the night. She spotted Dylan in the shadows amongst a small group of students.

He smiled when she came up beside him. "Hey, Aubrey, I'm almost done."

She blinked as he pulled hand-wrapped cigarettes from a plastic bag and handed them out in exchange for cash. "What are you doing?"

"Just being an entrepreneur." He flashed a confident grin.

"Are you selling?"

"Just pot." He folded the last of the cash into his pants and tucked the plastic bag back inside his coat pocket. "See, all done. Here, I saved us a couple." Dylan clinched one between his lips and extended the other toward her.

She didn't want to take it. But Aubrey liked the mellow high. Her cheater ex-boyfriend James never smoked pot or took drugs. In contrast to his bad-boy reputation, he was 'Mr. Clean', striving toward a football scholarship. Until dating Dylan, she'd never even considered smoking regular cigarettes, let alone the stash concealed in his coat.

Aubrey crinkled her nose. "Let's share. I don't wanna miss my prom." Again, the hollow sensation of déjà vu passed through her like a ghost from the past.

Dylan lit up and took a couple hits before handing it to her.

Aubrey inhaled and let it work its magic. As her thoughts drifted, she laughed at her parents' concern that James was the bad influence. She prepared to take another hit, but realized it had vanished from her fingers. Her head drooped down, thinking she'd dropped it. Then a hand lopped around her wrist.

She stumbled. "Hey, what's going on?"

"I'm taking you outta here," James snapped as he led her toward the parking lot.

"But I don't wanna go. I'm having a good time." She felt a chilly breeze brush past her.

Dylan appeared at the edge of the grass, just before the pavement. He yelled, "Let 'er go. She's with me."

Aubrey grinned with the thought that two guys would fight over her.

"Shove it. Out of my way," James shouted as he rammed his fist against Dylan's jaw. He dropped like a heavy sack to the ground.

When they reached his pick-up, James opened the door. He hoisted Aubrey up and scooted her across the seat as he slid in beside her.

"Where are we going?" she asked as the engine roared.

"Home." His gaze expressed an unpleasant reflection of his disappointment. "This isn't like you. I just don't want you getting hurt. I love you and always will," he said as they pulled out.

Aubrey rested her cheek against the cold glass, wondering if she'd changed that much since they'd been apart. James raced along the winding road. With the stars masked behind monstrous dark clouds, she could see no more than a few yards ahead.

In a flash, the pick-up's cabin filled with bright light from a truck approaching from behind, repeatedly honking its horn. They sped faster down the dark road. The mysterious truck banged their rear bumper. Aubrey's head snapped back. Her heart pounded.

"What the hell," James shouted. "Hold on."

She clutched the strap of her seatbelt. As the engine roared louder, she sensed them speed faster and faster, twisting further into the darkness. She glanced back. The truck inched closer and again smacked the rear bumper. Aubrey turned toward James. His face tensed. He jerked the steering wheel causing their pick-up to shimmy. His hand lunged across her chest and grasped her seatbelt.

She held her breath as the pick-up jumped the embankment. It tipped on its side and slid violently for several yards, snapping through numerous bushes. In a jarring crash, it stopped at the base of a tree.

The next thing Aubrey remembered was Dylan pulling her from the vehicle. She sat dazed in the grass near the wreck.

"Are you okay?" he asked.

"I think so." Though disoriented, Aubrey realized how lucky she was not to have been killed. She then noticed a smudge of blood across the front of her gown, but neither felt nor saw any open wounds upon her face or arms. She feared the blood to be that of James.

Dylan yanked her up by the wrist. "Come on. Let's go."

As he dragged her toward his truck, she glanced back. "What about James? Shouldn't we help him?" She again experienced the lingering emptiness in her stomach, this time more intense than earlier.

Dylan snapped, "He should've minded his own business. I'm already on probation. We need to get before anyone shows."

Aubrey's hand tightened on the door handle, vibrating as the engine revved. She considered that James might be seriously hurt, but didn't know what to do. The relentless empty sensation now consumed her. It veiled the sights and sounds of life around her.

"Come on. Get in," Dylan repeated in a hollow voice that seemed to have traveled from faraway.

At that moment her thoughts exploded in a montage of images and emotions. She began an unwanted journey through an imminent future she'd wished to forget.

The vision unfolded with James' family and friends gathered in the grass around his coffin. Aubrey's stomach twisted with the same guilt that prevented her from standing beside them at the church for the shared goodbye. The haunting image gave way to glimpses of endless parties where she drank and danced with abandon into the early morning hours. This lifestyle led to her parents kicking her out of the house. With nowhere else to go, she traveled with Dylan from cities to towns, selling drugs and taking odd jobs. She never craved more than another day.

As the years passed, Dylan showed her little respect. He frequently took other women to their bedroom while she lay barely conscious on the couch in their apartment . . . dreaming. If she talked back, Dylan responded with his fist or, if he was really angry, the baseball bat he'd stashed beneath the bed. But he would always apologize and shoot her up with the happiness that had become her only escape. In time, she no longer cared about the bruises, the broken bones, or the often painful swelling of her face and eyes.

Years of court-ordered rehab merely drew out the unpleasant memories of losing James. She wondered what direction her life might have gone had she made a different choice the night he died. Of course, after rehab, she'd return to Dylan.

In the end, Aubrey could muster no remorse the afternoon she found Dylan's lifeless body sprawled on the bed in their apartment. His face had been beaten into an unrecognizable bloodied mass. Her only concern being to find his stash and escape. At thirty-eight, she no longer desired to live. For her, life ended the day she killed James. That's how Aubrey remembered his death after she'd left him alone bleeding in his wrecked truck the night of prom. On that night, she felt that she too had died.

The vision ended its assault on Aubrey's senses, but her body continued to tremble. Her hand still gripped the handle of Dylan's truck. Scarcely able to catch her breath, she realized that James would die tonight. At prom, James asked her to give their relationship a second chance. But now, she was being offered a greater gift...a second chance for them both to live.

Dylan revved the engine and shouted out the open window, "Get in or I'm outta here."

She waved her hands and screamed, "Just go, LEAVE."

He laughed it off. "Suit yourself. You'll be back. I have what makes you happy." His tires spun the gravel and left behind a cloud of dust as he sped back toward town.

Aubrey found the strength to kick out the shattered windshield and pull James from his pick-up. She had dragged his bloody body halfway up the embankment when she heard an approaching car. Running alongside the road, she flagged it down.

On the drive to the hospital, Aubrey cradled his head in her lap. Her tears rained as she wiped the blood and dirt from his face. "James, I love you. This isn't how it was supposed to be."

She prayed that he wouldn't die, not tonight, not on her account. Aubrey loved him and wanted a second chance, a second chance at life. She kissed his lips and lingered in the moment before crying out, "Please, don't leave me. We were meant to be together...forever."

With a blink, the warm calm again enveloped her body and carried her through the tunnel of swirling white light.

Aubrey closed her eyes. She knew something had changed. Years of memories flowed through her like an endless river into a sea of joy. She weakly opened her eyes to the blurred image of James and her soul touched with clarity the love of those around her.

Beep...beep...beep sounded the heart monitor. The room seemed colder. James sensed the end was near. He squeezed Aubrey's hand when he noticed the sparkle of life return in her eyes.

"I love you," sprang from her lips.

Even after their fifty years of marriage, he still felt the power in those words. "And I you, my beloved. I could love no one more. I'm blessed. You saved my life."

She caressed his hand against her chest. Her tender gaze cut deep into his heart. "James, we were both blessed. You're my partner and my love. Together, we were given a second chance." Aubrey's grin took on a joyful glow before her glossy eyes relaxed and the monitor echoed a steady tonal cry.

"She's gone," the nurse whispered before silencing the monitor.

With a final squeeze of her hand, James shivered as tears streamed down his cheeks. Their children stood beside him, hands held and heads bowed in prayer.

Where had the years gone? He still pictured Aubrey as the spirited cheerleader who pulled him from the wreckage of his truck. Her smile greeted him when he awakened from his coma, two days after Dylan ran him off the road. Every day she slept in the chair beside his hospital bed while he stroked her thick golden hair. When their eyes met, he found strength in the words, "I love you." As he did tonight.

With the help of their son, James released Aubrey's hand and rose to his feet. He reflected on the early years of their marriage and the holidays spent with her parents. The love shared during those gatherings grew to include their children and grandchildren. He'd always cherish those memories.

Before leaving her to rest on this their final night together, James stood in the doorway of the hospital room and admired her once more.

"Forever my beloved," flowed from his lips.

James sensed the warm embrace of Aubrey's spirit and smiled. He'd always see her love in the lives of their children. In that way, she'd live on...forever in his heart.

ANDRES FRAGOSO JR.

Andres Frogoso, Jr. is innovative, strong, and full of surprises. His unique writing style and subject matter are an expression of his innermost wishes, hopes, dreams, goals, and, sometimes, secrets. The experiences of him being bi-polar, gay, Mexican American, and a bit crazy give him an interesting perspective of life. Each one of his aspects hold a unique fell to life. His struggles to keep his life balanced are only fortified by the love of his family that supports his eccentricities. Go to his website www.andresfragosojr.com, pull up a chair, get comfortable, and go through the website. Enjoy his poems, read his writing, and get a giggle from his blogs. You will have fun, and you will be glad you did. Enjoy.

Terradustria

Captain Beau Whitley opens the door of his Avian. His white, helmeted head sticks out in a deep contrast to the dark, burned fighter. He retracts his seatbelt and pulls himself out. His clumsy action causes him to drop fifteen feet to the ground, landing on his back. The heat from the fire leaking from the Avian approaches him. Beau slowly recovers from the shock of the crash and stands up, almost toppling over. In all of his ten years flying and fighting the Moralists, he had never had as close an encounter as this last one. This will be his first and last crash landing.

His first lieutenant's voice spoke loud in his ear, "BW? Do you copy?"

Beau takes his helmet off relieving him from the loud noise. With the helmet off, the voice was at a more comfortable audio range. He shakes his head and responds, "BW here."

"BW. Good, you are all right. I was worried there for a bit. Your vitals are not stable. You need to take an LSS shot, immediately."

Beau turned to look at his Avian. The crash landing caused the front magnets to fold against the hard ground. Fire was literally leaking from the other wing. "Chief Ju. That's not going to happen. I can't get in the Avian for the med kit."

"You must be in more shock than I anticipated. Use the emergency LSS on your flight suit. If you don't remember how to, I'll walk you through it, BW."

"Leave me alone, Chief Ju." Beau felt his jumpsuit for the firm disk on the right thigh. He slapped it hard and felt the adrenaline rush, with the other mix of medicines go into his blood system. The warm feeling of the opiate analgesic spread through his chest. Beau took a deep breath and held it as he landed hard on his knees and his forehead met the ground as in prayer.

"Take a deep breath, BW."

A few moments pass and Beau takes a deep breath and becomes fully alert. Standing up, he takes stock of his surroundings. The Avian broke the outer barrier of the plantation as planned.

"I'm at ground zero."

"Okay. Then, we will go to BZT25. Do you need a refresher?"

BW smiled at the sarcasm. "Just guide me there."

Beau followed Chief Ju's instructions through the old plantation to the mansion. "Chief Ju?"

"Yes, BW?"

"Have we done this before?"

"No. You're the first one to break the barrier in a hundred and seventy-five years. Why?"

Beau looks around the familiar grounds of the plantation mansion. It was a timeless, strong, southern plantation in the early 21st century. At the top of the landing, the front doors were missing. The staircase intimately curves around the four floors. The memories of southern bells dancing at their coming-out parties fill his head. He feels the need to move to the side and salute at the brave, young soldiers in confederate uniforms ready for the war re-enactment passing him by, others walking toward him. The sweet smell of pork barbecue wafts through the air. "Meat?" There was no such thing anymore. "Was that pork?"

"BW? What's going on? Your vitals are sporadic." After a short pause, Chief Ju asks, "Did you say pork?"

"It's like déjà vu. It's as if I've been here before. I can almost see the fat, old French cook in the kitchen roasting the hog, and the rest of the staff getting the dining room ready."

"What do you hear? You're vitals are going crazy."

"There's a live orchestra playing Chopin."

"That can't be. Our instruments show nothing, only your vitals. It could be holograms."

"I know. I don't understand it. I'm hallucinating."

"Technically, BW, you're not. The sounds seem real to you. Go to the main foyer and find the Grand Ballroom."

"I can almost taste the pork. I can smell the perfume from the roses, jasmines, junipers, and other flowers from the garden."

"That's impossible, BW. Don't let the holograms fool you. You need to reboot the system. If it stops, plants will grow again. Inferior animals will roam the world. Life as we know it will cease to exist."

"I know. I know. Stop hounding me."

Beau walks through the entire house. He knows every floor, every room as if he built it himself. The secret compartments and the hidden passages are easily distinguishable to him. In the attic, he moves a windowpane that opens and follows the secret passage straight down to the Grand Ball Room.

"BW? How did you know that was there?"

"I just know. I don't understand it."

Beau also knew where the main generator was located. It was breaking down. Some plants were starting to grow at the poles. The plants were causing changes to the climate, and the government would slow down. There were too many consequences if that happens.

"BW? What happened?"

"What do you mean?"

"Your vitals went off-line. We can't see anything in this room."

"Audio seems fine."

"You're not in the Grand Ballroom."

"I am."

"BW, we don't have much time. You need to reboot the system."

"Yes, Chief Ju. Yes, I know. You've already told me."

"I don't need to remind you of your mission, do I?"

Beau became puzzled at the comment. Why was Chief Ju so insistent on his mission? She was never like that before. It seemed as if they didn't want him to distract from the mission. The more he thought about it, the more confused he became.

As an orphan, the Minister of Mundovus had adopted him and loved him as a son, even if he is the most powerful man in the known, industrialized globe, Americus, and did not have time for him. When he became of age, he was coerced to enter the military, handpicked from among hundreds of Mundovus. It seemed unusual, his scores were high but not as high as many others who had more experience to do this mission.

"BW, you need to hurry. You only have twenty-five cycles to complete your mission. I can't stress the importance of this."

Beau was getting annoyed fast with Chief Ju's insistent voice in his ear.

"The free world depends on you doing this."

"Stop badgering me," Beau said firmly. "Why me? I don't understand."

"It's premature to tell you now." Chief Ju raised her voice. "Once you get to the Terradustria, I'll tell you." She took a moment and relaxed her tone. "Please, hurry. It's important."

Beau was perplexed. Why him? That one and only question bothers him more than anything else. The sound of the orchestra restarts, the scents of flowers emanates and the chatter murmurs once again.

"Find the damn thing and reboot it. NOW!"

Beau walks to the far wall, he stands face to face with a large portrait. He feels an icy sensation trail down his back, causing the hair follicles on his skin to stand on end. The room's temperature drops a few centigrades. The music stops, the chatter of the party ends, the smell of the flowers ceases. A sudden void of the senses envelops him. Beau, in disbelief, stares at himself in the portrait. No one had ever seen pictures of or any resembling the creator of the industrialized world, Dr. Beau Whitely. At the bottom of the portrait, a gold plaque revealed the name Dr. Beaumont Jonathon Whitley Fields. Beneath it stood a date, July 1, 2015, two-hundred years to the day. "Chief Ju?"

"BW, do your mission. That is an order."

Beau ignores the command. He sees the discoloration, the abandonment of the frame, dust all around. There should be cobwebs or animal droppings, the cotton eaten by rats. There was nothing like that. There were no animals in over a hundred years, or plants for just as long.

The portrait showed his dark brown, wavy hair. It was in style for the year, long enough to be above the bright, white shirt, barely touching the crisp collar. The bangs parted in the middle cascading into a frame of his long, masculine face in mid frown.

Subconsciously, he hand-combs his hair and blows at his bangs. He was past due for his regulation haircut. Chief Ju had been hounding him to get a haircut for the past three months. His excuse was he didn't have the time due to the training for this mission. His helmet had become a tight fit over the last few weeks.

Women always complimented his brows and long eyelashes. They would stare into his deep, brown, eyes. "What color are your eyes?" The grey-eyed girls always asked. They had never seen a color so rich and so dark. Everyone had grey eyes, but not him. "Chocolate," he would answer. He licks his lips savoring a distant memory of dark chocolate truffles from long ago. "Chocolate," he whispers.

"BW? What did you say?"

Touching his nose and looking at the portrait, he admires that the permanent down-sloping nose ends in a sexy bulb, very aristocratic for its era. Like his, it flows with his long face, giving him an air of nobility. No one had a nose quite like his. He didn't have children, so he never passed on that trait. Men look up to him. His nose commands attention and inspires jealousy. Three jealous men with flat, feminine noses had broken his as many times, which gave it more character.

Beau massages his jaw, how many combat fights has he been in? The long square jaw gave him a unique look. It ends with a semi-cleft chin, which made him look more virile and stronger than the rest of the men. "Caveman," the others called him. His physique was not unique, except that his body created strange gasses and smells, which at times were quite embarrassing.

"BW?"

Beau ignores the voice, entranced with the white, crisp shirt on the portrait. A match to his white uniform in style, even the collars were of the same height. The blazer on the portrait an exact replica of the burnt over-jacket of his uniform, designed for him. He pulls the lapels, straightens his shoulders, takes a deep breath, and pumps out his chest with pride. The portrait was that of him. "Nothing today would make me look this good."

"BW? What are you talking about? Get on with the mission."

Beau felt a trickle on his upper lip; he touches his nose and feels blood. He is bleeding. Again. The dry atmosphere always made him bleed. The background of the portrait was a soft brown with a swirled backdrop. Looking out the windows, the air was brown and swirly. It has always been like that. Memories of a blue sky with white clouds filled his head. The green of the grass and the multi-colored leaves of fall coloring his fields in different hues of red, orange, plum, purple, and yellow. He takes a deep breath and coughs. The air was getting moist. The increase of oxygen was affecting him, disorienting him.

"Captain Beau Whitely, are you with us?" Chief Ju's strong commanding voice was losing its force.

Beau raises his hand and passes it in front of the portrait, half expecting it to do the same. He felt stupid; it was a portrait. He lowers his head.

Suddenly, he hears a loud hiss. Streams of vapor escape the frame of the portrait. "Welcome back, Dr. Whitley," a soft, feminine voice said. The portrait began to move to the left leaving an opening exposed.

"BW? Are you there?"

"I'm here. I found the entrance."

Beau enters the familiar room. The pod in the middle with a few blinking lights is quickly deteriorating. Acid rain had seeped in making large gaps in the ceiling and in the walls. Concrete and steel were not enough to keep the Terradustria safe. "The Doctor didn't have the forethought of his invention," he said.

The door behind him closes with a loud thud, sealing him in.

"Chief Ju?" he asked.

The communication was lost.

"State your new name," the feminine voice said.

"Beau Whitley."

"Welcome back, Dr. Whitley. Please, hold for playback."

A screen in midair appears. It was sideways. The projector was malfunctioning. "Jenny, please adjust recording." Startled, he questions how he knew the name of the voice and what command to use.

The recording shifts, disappears, and then appears life size. The image of him, only older, appears. "Beau? They gave you my name?" The recording said.

"Yes. They gave me the original name."

"Warning, outer perimeter breached," Jenny said.

"What's that?"

"The Mundovus are approaching. They will not kill you, only stun your body in order to re-boot."

"What can we do?"

"You have to stop this. The world is dying slowly. If this continues for too long, the world as we know it will die. In a couple of hundred years, there will be no oxygen. I'm dying now, and it's only been forty years. The polar ice caps will melt. There will be no plants, no animals, and no hope."

"Why should I do anything?"

"You're me. I don't know what generation of me, but you're I. You were cloned because only I can reboot the system."

"That's what I'm here to do."

"Don't you remember anything? The oxygen? The water? The plants? The animals? The children?"

"The Mundovus won't let us know the past."

My daughter Jenny is barren and so is half her generation. The animals are dying, too."

Beau felt overwhelmed with memories, feelings of sadness and loss. "I remember. But how?"

"You're me, remember? You need to stop this. We need to stop this."

Beau felt a sudden need to save the world. "How?"

"Bleed on the patch." A small Petri dish came out of the side console. It had a small needle in the middle.

"What will that do?"

"I programmed a self-destruct system a year after. I saw my error. I was greedy. They stopped me. We need to do this."

"Warning. Warning." Jenny's voice was louder.

"BW? What are you doing?"

"Chief Ju?"

"I'm tapped into the receiver, as you can see, the seal is broken. Open the door. We need to finish this mission."

"Dr. Whitley. What will happen to me?"

"I have a protocol in place. Stay here, and they will pick you up. We'll fix the world, one man at a time starting with you. The world will change rapidly. Some will survive and return to normal or as normal as they can get. I don't know what the damage has been so far."

"I miss the taste of chocolate."

"Warning. Outer hall breached," Julie said.

"BW, I know you're in there. Open the door," Chief Ju yells. "It's an order."

Beau stands in front of the Terradustria. He didn't want to die. He opens his right palm and holds it above the Terradustria. A hissing sound came from his side. A large candy bar of dark chocolate lay in the middle.

"My favorite," Dr. Whitley said.

"It can't be. How?"

"You should know better. You're not the only human that eats organic material. There are things you don't know."

Beau thought about it. He never ate with anyone. His diet was always at home or specially made for his illness. "I'm not sick, am I?"

"No. You're the healthiest man on the planet."

"BW? Don't do anything stupid. We have one inch to go."

Beau could feel the heat from the door as it started to warp and turn red.

"Chocolate." It is not a question. It is not an answer. It is not a supplication. He picks up the bar and takes a bite. The bittersweet piece melts slowly in his mouth. An orgasmic feeling unlike any he had before. Confused by his erection, he takes another bite. It was just as orgasmic as the first one. His eyes widened, and a smile brightens his face. Another bite and yet another fills his mouth with pleasure. When the bar was gone, he walks over to the patch and slams his palm on the needle. He felt no pain, just pleasure. The Terradustria beeps and the remaining lights stop.

"Protocol BW is in place," Chief Ju said.

"Imagine that. The protocol has your name," Dr. Whitley said.

"What now?" Beau asked.

There was no answer. The lights in the room fade. Behind the console, a passageway opens. He ran and dove into it. As it closes, he hears the main door collapse. Chief Ju's last scream rang in his ear and forever locked in his memory. "Good-bye my friend, if you were my friend."

Beau ran through the dark passageway to the light at the end of the tunnel.

"Dr. Whitley, are you in there?" Jenny's voice said.

Beau came out by the dry riverbed. "I'm here." He looks around for a machine but found a young woman with brown eyes.

"Dr. Whitely?"

"Please, call me BW." Beau could not stop starring at the chocolate eyes on a beautiful woman with tanned skin and brown hair. "You're a Moralist."

"Yes, I am."

"You sound familiar."

"I'm Julie. I am a descendent of Jenny. She was your assistant."

"What now?"

"Finish what you started. Come on, we have to go."

Beau felt alive. He had a new purpose in life.

K. RAY KATZ

K. Ray Katz—"Writing is my hobby." Ray has written three novels, is currently working on a fourth, that deals with international politics, economics, or war. He's written several short stories, and this is the second time the Writer's Bloc anthologies chose one.

Prior to retiring, Ray had several careers: a Counter-Intelligence Agent working in the U.S., Europe, and Asia, a Theatrical Stage Manager in New York, a food distribution manager on the east coast, and the owner of a group of Audiology and Hearing Aid Dispensing offices in Arizona, along with a software development company. He and his wife call "The West" home, even though they enjoy traveling throughout the U.S. and Canada in a motor home, and visiting other countries each year when Henderson sidewalks get hot enough to fry an egg.

In the Name of Peace

The proposal was unprecedented—the consequences, should it become public knowledge—incalculable. But, the potential for either world peace or a renewed world conflict was not to be denied. To agree to it required a man of resolve, just as it had taken a man rooted in the realities and violence of a revolution to propose it.

The sequence of events leading up to the meeting had been put in motion with the Swiss being asked to use their "good services" as an intermediary. Even in the world of diplomacy, known for its secretive ways, the written note had been unusual in its brevity, as well as in the identity of its sender. Four follow-up notes had passed back and forth from their ambassador in Mexico City to the Swiss Ambassador, to the Mexican government, to his American counterpart, and on to the President in Washington, then back again to its originator before final arrangements were agreed to for the secret and undiplomatic meeting.

It was a cold, wet night in early March, not cold enough for snow, although it seemed too cold for rain. Winter's last gasp was making Washington residents miserable, yet again. Water was still dripping off the coat of the Russian Ambassador to Mexico as a Secret Service agent led him down a hallway to a door made different from all the others only by its number, B-232. It was the door to the President's private working office in the Treasury Building across the closed-off section of 17th Street, renamed West Executive Drive, just west of the White House. President Wilson's hide-a-way had seen its share of unusual meetings in the past year as the Great War had forced itself upon the nation, and yet, none more so than this one. A President simply did not meet with a representative of a country with which it did not have diplomatic relations; at least, not until lower level bureaucrats had worked through the many issues dividing the two countries. However, Woodrow Wilson had been so intrigued by what the notes had left unsaid, he agreed to the meeting which both countries would categorically deny ever having occurred.

To agree to work together for the common good, putting personal and ideological differences aside, was the essence of the proposal set forth in the letter, delivered directly into the President's hands by the Russian Ambassador to Mexico from Chairman Lenin. The two men were alone, not even an interpreter was present, although the Secret Service was just outside the door. It was war time. A large segment of the public had its roots in Germany and was having a difficult time thinking of the Kaiser's Army as their enemy, having until recently felt sympathy for Germany, while others simply hated the British. Soldiers with loaded Springfield rifles stood guard at every entrance to the building. The Ambassador said very little, and what he did was in slow, halting, broken English. He was clearly ill at ease with this unusual private meeting his Chairman had instructed him to arrange with the President of the United States. None of his aides had been involved, and he had requested the President maintain the same degree of privacy.

The President, ever the stickler for doing things properly, initially refused the request brought to him by Switzerland's Ambassador. It was a procedure that broke diplomatic protocol since it bypassed the Secretary of State. After the fourth request, Wilson finally acquiesced. His lack of enthusiasm at meeting privately with a representative of such a radical, blood-thirsty government was evident. However, his curiosity about what Chairman Lenin could want got the better of him.

Ambassador Golovny gave a quick bow as he entered the small room that was dominated by an ornate fireplace. The burning logs sat upon a pile of ashes showing the President had been at work for a number of hours. Even though he was physically tired, his clothes were wrinkle-free, his jacket buttoned, and his mind sharp.

In halting English, the Ambassador said, "Mr. President, Chairman Lenin has direct me I place letter in your hands only. With permission, I return in three week to receive your...re-response."

"And?" asked Wilson, expecting more to the meeting.

"I have complete my instructions. With your permission..." the ambassador gave another quick bow, turned and left the warm office to travel back to Mexico as a private citizen; his diplomatic status not being recognized in the United States. The President, surprised at the brevity of the meeting, remained standing for a moment, a thick envelope in his hand as he watched the door close.

The sealed envelope contained another, also sealed. When he convinced this tightly fitting envelope to reveal its contents, Wilson was able to read the thoughts of Vladimir Ilyich Lenin, whose handwriting and command of English was quite good. The thoughts of the Chairman were spelled out in clear, concise, unambiguous terms. Schooled in Russia and several other European countries, a world traveler and lecturer, the letter he wrote combined a unique view of world affairs and history along with what some might call his visionary thinking. Others would call his words an abomination. As to the accuracy of the conclusions he so clearly believed, history would be the judge. Whether or not he, Wilson, should agree with its conclusions and then act in concert with Lenin—that was the decision he was asked to make...must make!

"Mr. President, I take this unorthodox method of providing you with facts as I see them and the conclusions I have drawn from these facts." So started the letter presenting Lenin's view of Russia's precarious position in the world and why

it had been forced to arrange a separate peace treaty with Germany, leaving Great Britain, France, Italy, and now the United States to finish the war, putting the pragmatism of survival ahead of ideology. He continued discussing the shape of Europe and the world to come once Germany was defeated. He saw the world in both the immediate and the distant future based on several possible courses of action available to the Allies, all of which he was convinced would lead to another round of international blood-letting. In his opinion, there was but one course of action available to the victors that had a chance of guaranteeing peace and stability in Europe.

Lenin's proposal, stripped of any humanity or pretext of respectability, was for Russia and the United States, in the persons of their heads of state, to agree to do all that was in their power once the war was concluded to subvert the growth of the German people—including their industrial, artistic, economic, political, and military institutions. He acknowledged that such a concept was sure to be rejected by the noble-minded elements of world society, although the benefits of such a policy were too great to ignore.

He was convinced that the Germans were a militaristic people and would not learn from their defeat, and in the future, would again throw their hoards at their weakest neighbors unless prevented by a hard, unswerving policy of repression from the major countries of the world. If Wilson agreed with his premise, he, Lenin, planned to immediately embark on a campaign to convince other world leaders of the necessity of such action. He had decided to approach Wilson first. He was a well-known promoter of peace between neighbors, and without his active support, the plan had little chance of success. In effect, the success or failure of the idea, as well as the shape and structure of peace in Europe, was likely to depend upon a decision made by the President of the United States, a man who had done everything in his power to keep his country out of European affairs.

Wilson accepted, without question, the request put forth by Lenin that the contents of the letter must never be divulged to anyone other than himself, his direct successors and other like-minded heads of state. To do otherwise would inevitably lead not only to political ruin, but to an outcry by the civilized peoples of the world unequaled in modern times. But, was this the way to build international trust and cooperation? To accept as gospel the idea that Germany could not, or would not learn from the folly of the war that had taken the flower of its youth and once defeated, would again rebuild its military and use armed force to seek more land and power?

The idea of espousing the brotherhood of man on the one hand, and on the other doing everything possible to prevent the German people from rising above the most basic human concerns of food and shelter was monstrous. As much as he abhorred it, Wilson had to admit, however grudgingly, that it might have merit. He could not deny the Allies, as Lenin had suggested, were destined to win the war even without Russia's help. Once committed, America, with its industrial strength and military, was in it to the end. However, was it in the best interests of both Russia and the United States, or just Russia, to promote a weak Germany which was, after all, the center of Europe in so many ways other than merely geographic? To Wilson, a new democratic Germany, economically viable and politically stable, was preferable to any other alternative. The problem with this outcome was the German people. Their prosperity seemed to fuel their war-like nature, overshadowing many laudable achievements.

It was a decision that he must make with care and on the merits of the case itself. He must divorce the decision from his own humanitarian instincts and decide solely on what was best for his country—his people. That was the reason he had been elected President. To make the hard decisions on behalf of his countrymen who had placed their trust in him when he had sworn to *protect and preserve*.

How simple the job looked when he ran for office. How complicated it really was! He tapped the letter on the table beside him as his mind wandered while gazing at the glowing embers in the fireplace before him. Did he have the right to join in an act that he must keep secret from those closest to him? Should he work in concert with a Bolshevik government that one day might be America's enemy, the antithesis of what his country stood for?

The answers would not be simple ones! Lenin had asked for an answer by the end of the month as Wilson's decision was bound to have a great bearing on future relations between Russia, the German Kaiser, and other world leaders. The President knew he needed at least that much time to arrive at the right decision. Lenin, in the conclusion of his letter, had stated that *"peace took many forms and that the meaning of the word must be determined by each man for himself."*

In the name of peace, should he promote the national stagnation of another country on such an immense scale? Truly—that was the question Lenin had put to him. To act in contradiction to everything the United States stood for, to intentionally cause women and children to starve, to make men grovel for the barest necessities, to make the mere act of survival so difficult that people, no matter their inclination, would never have the means to threaten their neighbors. Then, having done all that, what might these same people do if their burden was lifted from their shoulders and allowed to once again become a powerful nation?

Wilson's humanitarian upbringing and legal background made him abhor the consequences of agreeing with Lenin, while his strong desire for a lasting peace prevented him from rejecting it out of hand. As he neatly folded the letter and placed it back inside its two envelopes, Wilson knew, as much as he wanted to ignore it, he must decide upon an answer.

The weight of his unmade decision was visible in his every step as he walked back to the White House and climbed the three flights of stairs to his waiting bed. Beginning tomorrow, in the name of peace, he would seek his advisors' unwitting counsel to help him determine the future of the German people.

JUDY SHINE LOGAN

Judy Shine Logan is an accomplished writer, public speaker, and Masters level educator who currently serves as the Librarian/Historian for the Henderson Writers' Group. For over twenty years, Judy designed and developed training curricula for a major healthcare company. She also created and delivered a GED Preparation curriculum for a New Hampshire school system for 5 years before relocating to Las Vegas in 2010.

Her recent fiction credits include the novel *Shelter Me: When friendship is all that remains* (Ink and Quill Publishing, November 2013); two short stories published in *WildflowerMagazine* (February and July 2011, www. wildflowermagazine.com); a short story scheduled for publication in *ChicaPeeps Women's Anthology* (http://www. chicapeeps.com); and a short story published in Writer's Bloc IV (2012) (http://mysticpublishers.com).

Judy has three grown children and a feral cat named "Pretty Girl".

The Black Box

"I want a friendship ring," I demand. "We've been going together for two years."

"Is that right?" he says.

"You know it is. All my girlfriends in school have friendship rings, and I'm the only one with a boyfriend and no ring!"

"I'll have to think about a friendship ring," he nods, watching me. "But, I did bring you something...."

I pout for a few seconds. "What?"

"This," he smirks, handing me a long plastic tube with some god-awful thing inside.

"What the heck is this?"

"Open it," he taunts me.

Gingerly, I pull the ugly creature from the tube and nearly drop it. A wrinkled, rubber-faced vulture head sits upon a fuzzy purple body on top of a single-taloned foot.

"Ewwww..." I say dropping the critter.

He laughs, picks it up, and hands it back to me. "Read the sign in its mouth."

Cranky and disappointed, I read it aloud in sing-song fashion: "Don't be sad, don't be blue 'cause I'm the bird who'll worry for you."

Tears welled up in my eyes. "That's so...touching," I say, not sure that's the right word to use.

"Look inside the tube, again," he insists.

At the bottom of the lair lays a black box. I looked up at him in confusion.

"Go ahead, get it."

I dig my fingers into the tube, but the cylinder is too narrow to reach the bottom. I turn it over and shake it until the black box plops into my hand.

Confused, I look at him. "What is this?"

"Open it for heaven's sake."

I hold the box firmly in my right hand and lift its cover with my left. "Oh, my gosh! It's gorgeous..." I cry.

He reaches over, takes the box from my hand and removes the engagement ring, slipping it onto my finger. "Will you let me be the bird who worries for you?"

"Yes, I will." I cry.

And he has. For thirty-eight years, he has taken care of me and our children, just as I have taken care of him -- a partnership—at least, until today.

"Bird," I say.

You don't move in the bed. Your eyes are closed, your breathing is shallow, and your skin is yellowing. I can't tell if you are conscious.

"Bird," I say again.

"Yeah, yeah," you finally answer me.

My heart leaps. I look for your eyes to open, but they don't. You remain still. Only the ticking of the clock breaks the silence.

I don't know how to begin. "I talked with the kids last night, and..."

Oh God, this is so hard.

I choke as tears gush from my eyes and my throat closes up. I can't stop sobbing.

Finally, I begin, again. "Bird."

"Yeah, yeah," you answer, though your eyes remain closed and you do not incline your head toward me.

My hand is shaking as I reach for yours—the strong muscular hand that has fed us all these years...strong even now, though it's missing the finger they took a month ago.

I lift your hand to my lips and the blanket falls away

from your chest. I see the scars, again—like railroad tracks carved into your flesh. There are so many of them. I can barely stand it.

At my touch, you finally move, though reflexively, and the blanket outlines the stump where your leg lived only last week. I cannot bear it, anymore.

"Bird, I'm going to stop your dialysis and let you go," I say, condemning you to death and me to widowhood.

For long minutes, I sob into the silence.

Suddenly, you speak. "God bless you, Judy."

I nearly faint. I look at you, willing your eyes to open, praying that you forgive me for letting you die. Your eyes remain closed, and you don't speak again for long, long minutes.

"Ok, hon, get going," you say.

I can't move from the bed, or stop crying.

Without opening your eyes or turning toward me, a second time you say, "Ok, hon, get going."

Confused, I plead, "Bird, where do you want me to go?"

"You go to heaven, and I'll find you there."

You forgive me.

Now, I am looking down on your peaceful, unmoving face as you lay dead in the black walnut box. "Thank you, Bird, for everything," I whisper as I kiss your face for the last time. "I love you, and I'll see you in heaven, soon. I promise."

WOLF O'ROURC

Maybe he hails from the American Midwest. With Wolf, you can never tell. So far, he has called 16 dwellings around the world home, giving his writing a cosmopolitan flair. His varied interests led to jobs in totally unrelated fields. Psychologists may diagnose him with ADHD, AADD, ADAD, or some other newfangled name, but really, he probably just cannot make up his mind. Makes for interesting reading, though. Wolf currently lives in a quiet, boring little town nobody knows, Love Vegas.

And the Winner Is ...

Sunday. Election Day in Berlin. Did the grand plan work? Had it been enough? All the effort, the struggle, the big show, the shouting, the raised fists, the tweets and posts, the millions on Alexanderplatz, one of the most fabled places of the city. It's all about the numbers. It's always about the numbers. Had the young people come out to deliver victory, despite all the naysayers? What do these narrow-minded, so-called pundits know, anyway? Everybody laughed at the idea of me becoming Chancellor. They laughed at Hitler, too, back then, in the last century, in 1925.

The polls just closed. Any second now the first official projection will come in. All eyes are glued to the screens in the ballroom decked out in green bunting.

Unofficial whisper numbers came in all afternoon. Actually, nobody told me. In the age of social media why bother with something as antiquated as talking? Supporters merely come over and show me their smartphones. They display a bar chart, lines, or simply a number. What's the visual equivalent to whispering? Blindness? Semi-blindness? Low light, like dusk or dawn? I've got it! They've been showing me twilight numbers, but they are not showing me what I need to see, what I'm clamoring for.

Across the ballroom I spot one of the party chief talking to Çem, the state legislator from Kreuzberg. He turns his head for a brief moment and gives me a thumbs up. Well unspoken. It's all his fault.

Two years ago I was a nothing, too young to be taken seriously. Sure, I talked a good talk in the election district. Had great rapport, especially with the young ones. Twitter, WhatsApp, meinVZ, Vimeo, Pheed, you name it, I'm on it. You only need to speak their language and know what they want, deep inside. The old folks don't. I do. I connect. I entertain. Young people listen when I talk. Still, the youth of this country, any country, doesn't vote, doesn't participate. So, I was a nobody. Bad numbers.

Now everyone knows my name, even if those saboteurs in the press get it wrong. They call me "Adolf" and other insults, everything from empty airhead to dangerous demagogue. As if Hitler had a monopoly on amusing speeches. What about those Italian clowns whose names escape me right now. I mean, like, they discovered this sh... stuff. Flamboyant gestures, animated facial expressions, dramatic language have been around since before Roman times. So have manipulation, propaganda, and demagogy. Hitler did not invent them. Calling a good speaker "Adolf" is like calling a good mouser "Tiger." Totally exaggerated and unfair. Besides, unlike me, *Adi*, as I like to call him, did not do it all himself. First, he stole his trademark moustache from Charlie Chaplin. He also had lots of help from his Propaganda Minister, Josi. Goebbels gave some of the best, well-known speeches, but was not half as good looking or popular with the kids as Der Führer. They like someone straightforward. Someone who tells the truth and keeps his campaign promises. Adi may have bent the former, but he sure kept the latter. At least, the big ones, like land in the East and a Volkswagen in every driveway. Okay, so his wars kind of, sort of led his plans astray. Not my concern. I never made such huge promises, nor did I want to conquer the world. I was asked to run by Çem.

Something funny about letters with appendages, where you have to look very carefully. That little hook under the "C" makes all the difference. Adds a "T" to the "sh." *Tshem* with the little thingy dangling from the front asked me for an alliance. Actually, he called it an axis. Like Germany and Turkey had an axis during World War I. Held for four long years, same as a term in the legislature.

Nobody knows the final numbers, but youthful volunteers scurry around the ballroom handing out little flags and balloons, just in case. The energy and exuberance of that age bracket made my career, made me.

The Green party had always dominated parts of the city center, then pushed to the East. Now Çem wanted to extend the axis south. Lots of young voters down there, those that appreciate straight talk, like the "Straight Talk Express" of one of the US presidential candidates way back when. Didn't do him much good, though. He needed more than the truth and campaign promises — youth, vigor, the Internet, social media, showmanship, and the numbers. I have all that. So Çem asked me for an axis for the Berlin State Parliament. Yes, Berlin is a city and a state, and not a small one at that. Three and a half million citizens. Big numbers with a big legislature.

Sounded like a good idea back then, even though I had no chance of winning. The Reds and the Blacks split the vote in the southern districts. Then the conservatives didn't like being black anymore and changed their color to orange. Now the Reds and the Oranges split the vote in the southern districts, but pay and perks of four k a month made a convincing argument. And I always said, if you dream, dream big — state legislator, federal legislator, Minister, Chancellor, Führer. Why not? Besides, it sounded like fun. What did I have to lose? I starred in my own version of *The Candidate*, free to say whatever I wanted. Then a funny thing happened on the way to the Berliner Forum. The young crowd got all excited about one of theirs running their way, all high-tech with texts and tweets and other cool things. The local starving artists threw their weight behind me and produced some of the most entertaining videos the Net had ever seen. They won me thousands of followers. In turn, my youth army's get-out-the-vote efforts won me a seat. It's all about the numbers.

I became the miracle man, the eighth wonder of Berlin politics. So started my story-video ascent to national fame, a rise that brought me right here, into a ballroom decked out in green. On my left, a talking head suddenly appears on the monitor. He doesn't release me from my excruciating ignorance.

On my right, Sepp Kuglhofer suddenly appears on the linoleum. "You're excited?"

Is he kidding? I'm dying. Where are those damn numbers? Although, I shouldn't care. I don't have a grand vision. No Lebensraum in the East. No great empire. No Volkswagen in every driveway. I don't even own a car. Like most Berliners, I rode the subway until recently. After the *challenge* with my brand of humor, I needed a bullet-proof car. One of my rap videos went viral. Gosh, it was only a joke! Obvious from the exaggerated expressions, wild color scheme, and overwrought music. The kids loved it. Millions of hits. The press called me "Adolf." Millions of curses. The left pilloried me. The right got all indignant. And the center, well the center is in the boring center. They must be Prussians. Prussians have no sense of humor.

Kuglhofer slaps my back. Kuglhofer. Such a funny word, like anything from the South. Bavarian names are hilarious. They can't help it. Don't even get me started on the Austrians. LOL. Prussian names are not funny. How can they be? I'm sure there's a law that you have to fill out a form in triplicate every time you say one. Prussians invented bureaucracy. Nothing to laugh at. No wonder none of the politicians up North enthuse and entertain. How can they? Comedians know the value of a funny name. Prussian politicians do not. They lull the electorate to sleep when they open their mouths. Kind of limits the voter turnout to the percentage of sleepwalkers.

Kuglhofer understood that, naturally. He has a funny name and he comes from the land of beer and honey. Bavarians invented fun. Unfortunately, that's why they kept losing wars to the Prussians. No fun. The South got its revenge in the end, however. Ten euros for one Oktoberfest beer. No fun for those damned tourists from the North.

Anyway, he approached me six months ago, in one of his less drunk moments. I had to run for the Bundestag, the federal parliament, high up on the list, where I could do the party some good. Germans cast two votes, one for a candidate, and one for the party list. Weird system that started after the disaster named *Adi*, but it makes for huge coattails in elections. Popular leading candidates on the list let a party rake in second votes and hence more seats. Pulling in the youth vote the way I did, they had to take me. Call it blackmail, if you like. Kuglhofer is good at that, and he has a funny name.

The rest is history. The Greens practice basis democracy, as they call it. Big mistake, if you don't like the so-called majority opinion. Helped out Adolf, if you know what I mean. I needed a top spot on the state party list, one that guaranteed a seat in the Bundestag, even if I lose the candidate vote. Power, money, influence, the public lime light, the numbers. Well, my young supporters full of zest and zealotry showed up for the nominating conventions. Guess who got the top spot? Actually, I got the second spot in the state. Party rules prohibit men from running for the top spot in Berlin, and I abhorred a sex change, but I'm top dog for the big prize. I head the national ticket. Normally meaningless for one of the smaller parties, as the Greens never get enough votes to designate the chancellor, but weirder things have happened. Lucky for me they also loath uniforms. Adolf got away with a sea of brown outfits. Can you imagine the same in green? On national television? This ballroom already puts me too much in touch with my inner forest.

The top spot guaranteed a minister post. Thirteen k a month. Not bad for someone who cares more about partying than politics. Then it happened. The crazy, over-the-top video. C'mon, it was a joke. They should allow do-overs. Golfers can take Mulligans, why not politicians? Calling me "Adolf" was the least of the insults from the intelligentsia. Unfair, if you ask me. Adolf would never have stood for publication of those incendiary, mean-spirited commentaries. The reporters would have disappeared beforehand. Did I stoop so low? No, but I showed them, anyway.

My young guns organized a rally, a big one on Alexanderplatz, the site of many historic demonstrations. One hundred fifty thousand people showed their support for poor, misunderstood me, the police said. I wonder how they even figured that out. The cops don't actually count the people. I'm sure more of my supporters filled the plaza. The police probably just have a contest. A lieutenant waving euro bills in his hands takes bets from officers making guesses. He shouts numbers to a sergeant, who puts them up on the board. Majority rules. Or the chief just picks a figure that lets his friends make the big bucks. Crooks, all of them. I'm sure more than two hundred thousand voters came to watch my show that day. Half a million went to the big demonstration of civil rights activists that brought down the Berlin Wall, and they came nowhere close to my poll numbers. No, the police had it wrong. I saw at least three hundred thousand cheering me on. Until I came on stage.

The clatter of my champagne flute shattering on the polished ballroom floor rips me out of my reminiscing. Kuglhofer gives me a funnier look than usual. What does he know about fear? He never had to face a humongous horde in defense of his honor, fighting for political survival, for everything, like I did, slave to the numbers, months ago, on that stage, facing Alexanderplatz.

What an entrance I made back then. Total silence filled the place holding four hundred thousand when I emerged from behind the curtain in a light brown uniform and cap, matching tie, leather belt with shoulder strap, and red brassard around my left upper arm. The obligatory black toothbrush moustache provided the finishing touch. The baggy black pants and shoes didn't fit, but the podium hid them. I spent much time making the rest look exactly like Adolf's uniform, and the meaning was not lost on the half a million waiting in the sun. You could have heard a dozen pins drop when I made the Hitler salute, the real one he used, arm upright, not the tedious one he decreed for his minions, made with outstretched arm. Then, the show started.

"*Volksgenossen* and *Volksgenossinnen*," I greeted the six hundred thousand strong crowd, as I unbuckled the belt and slowly twirled it like any good stripper would.

"Let's not dwell on the misfortune of the past weeks, but look forward to a brighter future full of glee." The leather garb flew into the crowd. A few of the seven hundred thousand strong got the picture and cheered, as I struggled out of one arm of the jacket, not without lewdly flashing the white shirt a few times first.

"But..." I pried off the red armband and raised it to the sky, then dangled the trophy suggestively in front of the million assembled, moving it slowly from left to right. Hands reached for it.

"We have to do this *together*." The clothes flew into the crowd of one and a half million. I slipped out of the jacket, held it high, and shouted, "Who's with me?" So what if I stole the line from Bluto in *Animal House*. He made it to US Senator, didn't he? The two million listening with bated breath responded like I knew they would. Laughter and shouts of "*Ich, Ich*" erupted from all sides.

A melee of hands grabbed for the heavy jacket. I don't know who won the tug of joy. My voice rose. "Do you believe with me in the final total amusement of the German people?" The military cap did its best impression of a Frisbee before diving into the waiting arms of two and a half million raucous revelers.

"Are you and the German people willing to party, if the Führer orders, ten, twelve, and if necessary, fourteen hours a day and to give everything for joy?" Whistles and boisterous laughter came from the three million following my every word when I slipped into a tight black coat held by my assistant.

"Do you want total fun?" I screamed. The curtain behind me fell, revealing a banner spouting "TOTAL FUN— LONGEST FUN." A humongous roar set Alexanderplatz a thunder. "If necessary, do you want fun more total and radical than anything that we can even imagine today?" Cries of "*Spaß, Spaß*—fun, fun" boomed toward me.

The grand finale, which I had practiced for days. A black bowler in hand, I flipped it onto my arm, snapped my elbow, and sent the hat sailing onto my head. The crowd of three and a half million went wild. That's all the people in Berlin. Take that you Wall-crumbling, civil-rights-hugging activists of days gone by. I now own Alexanderplatz, this city, this nation.

My assistant slapped bushy eyebrows onto my face and handed me a cane, thus completing the transformation to Charlie Chaplin's Tramp. Even the last of the jaded four million got it. "Now, people, rise up and let the party break loose!"

A chant started in the crowd and swelled to a chorus of five million, the same phrase that brought down the communist regime of East Germany with one tenth that number. "We are the people! We are the people!"

I raised my fist clutching the cane into the sky. "To Election Day and beyond!" Okay, I admit I stole that one from *Toy Story*, a movie popular among the young ones. What do you expect? I have to cater to my childish fan base.

Various social networks broke down during my grand speech. No wonder, with six million enthusiasts hammering their smartphones at the same time. The news had to pick up the—

Kuglhofer nudges me and points his funny, short finger at a monitor. Colored bars race horizontally across the screen, one showing the number from the last election, and the other the count for today. The second one keeps going and going. My head is ready to explode. The dreaded moment of truth. All or nothing. A voice expresses surprise at the huge number. The tension releases. Victory. Thanks to the enormous enthusiasm of the young people, the winner of this election is the voter with a heretofore unheard of turnout of 95.7%. Who says elections aren't fun?

KEVIN B. PARSONS

Kevin Parsons wrote *Ken Johnson and Roxi the Rocker*, a children's book. He's been published in numerous magazines and the *Las Vegas Review Journal*. He was also a contributing writer to *Seeking God First*, an anthology of devotions, and *Pursuing Your Passions* with Judi Moreo. He has also tested products and written reviews for *American Motorcyclist Magazine*. He wrote *50 Stories in 50 States*, a five book series of short stories, inspired by the recent journey with his wife, 50 states in 50 weeks on a motorcycle. The books are available on Smashwords.

River Dreams

*My wife and I rode a motorcycle across America, visiting
every state. I wrote short stories of the culture of each one.
This short, Illinois, is one of fifty.*

*Riding along the Mississippi River, I saw why so many
people have written about it. I got to imagining what kind of
a youth would be spent in a rowboat, up and down the river
… with a bit of adolescent love thrown in, of course.*

In 1959, I learned on the Mississippi River that life isn't
fair. My dad, in a wonderful and unexpected show of
being human, allowed me to use the rowboat that summer.
We'd just gotten out of school for the summer, and Quincy
Elementary School saw the last of me until September. As
the principal rang the bell for dismissal, I hit the back door
and didn't look back.

"Bobby, you're going to be an adult soon," Dad said,
"so you need to enjoy yourself this summer. Marcia is old
enough to take care of herself, so you can get out on the
river with the rowboat a bit. Probably won't get a chance
like this again."

Incredulous and afraid he'd change his mind, I asked
him how far I could take it.

"As far as you like. Upriver or down. But be home on
time for dinner or I'll warm your butt." I knew the threat
to be real.

I lay in bed that night and stared at the ceiling, unable to sleep, thinking of the great adventures ahead. I'd go upriver first, thinking if time got to be a problem, I could make time downstream a lot easier. The next morning I set out with Johnny Ray. We made an agreement that I would row upstream and he would take us back. Since he was two years younger than me, it seemed fair.

That year Ritchie Valens' 'Oh, Donna' made the top of the hits. I must have played that song a thousand times on the record player. Mom owned a couple of records, Pat Boone and Bing Crosby. She got an Elvis Presley album too, but hid it from Dad. He said the guy was too sexy, something like that. We listened to him together, and I thought he was real good. Dad hated my music, too, so I only played it when he was at work. My favorite song was 'Mack the Knife' by Bobby Darin. I didn't understand all the words, but the beat was really neat. Something about a tug boat, so it must be on the river. Look out, old Mack is back.

It stuck in my head as we headed out the first day with a sack of peanut butter sandwiches and two Cokes that Johnny Ray stole from his dad. Neither one of us lived on the river, so we carried the boat between old man Crenshaw's house and the Boysen twins' place, older girls who never knew we existed. Crenshaw caught us and asked us what we were doing. After we told him, he said we could keep the boat at his dock. It must be the moon or something, but mean old men were suddenly all becoming nice.

Our simple life just got simpler.

I held the boat for Johnny Ray as he climbed in. "So how long can you stay out?",

"My dad don't care if I ever come back."

I put the oars in the oarlocks. *His dad doesn't care? He sounds more like Huckleberry Fin than I do.* "Tell you what, Johnny Ray, you can be Huck Finn, and I'll be Tom Sawyer."

"Really?"

"Yep."

"Keen."

I rowed out a bit and we embarked on Day One of a three-month adventure into the river, the forests, and life full of adventures and heartbreak.

I rowed upstream and Johnny—that is, Huck—held onto both sides as we glided past the park, under the railroad trestle, and up to Earel Camp Road. The sun beat down and I took my shirt and shoes off. Twice, Johnnie Ray and I jumped in the water after beaching the boat. I couldn't take my eyes off that boat for fear I'd lose it, and worse yet, lose the precious freedom my father granted to me.

The sun beat down relentlessly as we ate our lunch that first day, entirely too early. We sat in a clearing with mud dried to our ankles from the gooey mess that ran from the river to firmer ground. In '59, the river ran low from the drought.

"Tomorrow we bring fishing poles."

Johnny Ray spoke around a huge gob of sandwich. "Don't got one."

"I got two." I'd take Marcia's. She never used it. Being eleven, she steered toward dolls. I scanned the area. "We need to find a good tree. Bring a rope and make a gigantic rope swing. Bigger than Danny Arlens'."

"Think we can?"

"Sure."

Johnny Ray rowed back while I fretted about the time. The first day and I better not be late. We tied the boat at Crenshaw's dock and I ran home. I crashed through the back door with Johnny Ray in my wake. Mom stood at the oven with a mitt on and pulled out a fresh batch of cookies.

"What time is it?"

She set the sheet down and looked at her watch. "Almost 1:30. Would you like a cookie?"

Johnny Ray said, "Sure." We sat at the table and I smacked my forehead.

We arrived four and a half hours early.

Each day we got better. We learned our lesson and left our shoes at home. We wouldn't put them back on until the first day of school, when we discovered they didn't fit. I rowed farther, Johnny Ray rowed upstream some, and we packed provisions, including rope, fishing poles, my b.b. gun, matches, knives, butter, more and more food, and tackle. We found a great spot to stash much of it, at a nice landing place. We caught fish and fried them for lunch. Our expeditions got bigger, too, as we ventured to the Iowa side of the river, avoiding the huge barges that slid by. But mostly, we stuck to the Illinois side and discovered more territory upstream, Lewis and Clark searching out the forests and fields. Inland, we found an oak tree that we could climb, so high we could see the surrounding landscape. I could, anyway. Johnny Ray didn't get that far up. We built a huge rope swing on the river's edge, too. The attachment to the tree took courage, as I crawled out the massive branch and kept inching out as the branch got thinner. Three times I fell off into the water, and the third time, it knocked the wind out of me. I struggled to the beach and flopped on my back, gasping for air.

Johnny Ray looked at me, choking and heaving, his eyes huge. "Maybe, we should try a smaller tree. Not so far up."

I struggled to my feet. "No way. This is the tree." I climbed again and got it tied.

The swing, being so long, took a long time and a lot of pushing and swinging to reach its arc, but after numerous times I could fly. The wind blew in my face and back, and at full arc I could see way up and downriver. At the full extension, I'd jump into the river. Old Huck wouldn't get it swinging so much. I tried to push him higher, but couldn't get him high enough. He needed to pump his legs to help, but he would have nothing of it. No matter how much I teased him about being a chicken, it yielded no better results.

Each day we went farther, creating places for different activities. Past the Earel Camp Road, we set up a fort and played cowboys and Indians. Upstream a bit, we found an eddy where the fishing was good. Two hundred yards deeper, we discovered a meadow where we cleared out a spot for lunch. Maybe a half mile more and we found a beach where we brought our Tonka truck and loader (both mine, he didn't have any) and we built roads, cities, and pools that fed from the river. We developed a routine that got us home later and later. Three times that summer I arrived home late for supper, sure my dad would break out the belt, or a switch, or his hand. He just frowned and said, "A little late tonight, aren't you?" The third time he took away my dessert and ate it himself, lemon meringue pie. Ever since then, I can't seem to get enough lemon meringue pie.

As we extended our borders and traveled farther upriver, we—that is, I—discovered Sandra Thompsen. Bored with the trucks, I suggested we row up a bit more. Johnny Ray climbed in and sat on the front of the boat, his legs hanging into the water. I rowed upstream, my strokes smooth and powerful, as the boat and we learned the ways of the water together. As I paddled close to the shore looking for snakes or frogs, we hit a clearing with a house. I spotted her on the deck in a chaise lounge chair. Sandra.

The clouds parted and the sun shone on her straight blond hair, and the music came up. None of that happened, but it might as well have. She was at an angle and leaned back on the chair, wearing shorts and a T-shirt. She wore blue shorts, had long tanned legs, her shirt a dazzling white. The sun bleached her hair to a bright blond. I stopped rowing and stared. Sandra was two grades ahead of me and in high school. I hadn't seen her in two years. Those years had been good to her. She developed curves and shapes that transformed her from a gawky girl into a goddess. I turned the boat around and hoped she didn't see me. Johnny Ray sat up with the changing motion.

"What's going on?" he looked around.

"Nothing. Just going back down a bit," I whispered.

"I thought we were going to try to get up to Bay Drive."

"Not today."

"Okay. Let's go back and play trucks."

I kept my voice low. "Naw, I don't want to do that." I prayed she didn't hear our conversation.

"Cowboys and Indians in the inlet then."

I just wanted to think about Sandra.

I rowed to her place alone. Tied the boat to her dock and sauntered up to her deck. Today, fully prepared, I wore a white shirt untucked with the top button unbuttoned. Sandra lay on the chaise lounge, sleeping. She wore the same outfit, blue shorts and white top. Her arms were tanning nicely.

"Hello, Sandra."

She sat up, startled. "Bobby." She brushed her beautiful golden locks away from her face and dazzling green eyes.

"Mind if I sit down?"

She patted the flat part of the chair beside her.

I sat so close our hips touched. She smelled like lilacs. "I saw you row past the other day."

"You did?"

She nodded and closed her green eyes for a second. A dozen freckles graced each cheek. Full lips with a hint of lipstick. "I've been thinking about you ever since."

"I have, too. I've bee—"

She kissed me. She put her long, slender fingers behind my head and pulled it to her face.

That's the scene I rehearsed in my mind, every day, a thousand times that summer. The blue and white outfit. The hair, brushed back. The kiss. A thousand times. Maybe, more. Yet, I never spoke to her, and she didn't know I existed.

We didn't mean to take the boat out every day that summer, Johnny Ray and I. Lots of times we'd play hopscotch or find other kids and played tag or Red Rover, but the sun would get up in the sky and beat down on us. We'd take off, and the other kids would beg us to bring them along. But their parents forbid it. We would launch as the big men in the neighborhood, and by the time we floated past Sandra's house, we transformed into little boys.

After the first chance meeting, I made sure we rowed past her house every day. Most days she didn't appear, the star of the stage leaving the hungry crowd of one wanting more. But once in a while, she would appear as we cleared the trees, sunning, watering flowers, or lying in the hammock. That was the worst, as I could barely see her.

One day we glided past as Sandra played croquet with her mother. She bent over the ball, the mallet in her hands, and her backside to us. An amazing view. She wore polka dotted shorts, blue on white, and her tan legs accented that outfit in an amazing display of beauty. Her mom said something and she laughed a high, carefree, lilting laugh that changed me. If I could make her laugh like that with me, it would be a time of blissful peace and harmony. We would both laugh together.

"Hey, man, row," Johnny Ray said.

The boat drifted toward their dock. I back paddled hard while trying to be quiet. Imagine if we crashed into her dock. Then I'd look idiotic. I aimed the boat downstream and let him row.

He steered the boat to Pirate's Island, which wasn't an island, just a bit of a sandy beach. Johnny Ray got a scarf and tied it around his head. He put his hands on his hips and said, "Arr." He looked silly.

I decided I would go up to Sandra's place the next day. Alone.

Because I couldn't think of a good reason to tell Johnny Ray he couldn't come, I just took off early by myself. I packed a lunch and some bait. And I brought my best white shirt. Pirate's Island appeared out of the morning mist. I stopped there and practiced. "Hello, Sandra. I'm Bobbie. I've been rowing past your house this summer…"

No.

"Hi, Sandra. I couldn't help but see you."

No.

"Sandra. Would you like to go for a ride in my boat?"

Better. Then I would be offering her something.

I wrote her name in the sand with a stick while practicing my lines and carving our initials in a tree with a heart surrounding them. I tried to practice holding her hand, but holding my own didn't work. At last I stood, and working up my courage, got in the boat and paddled to her house. Right as the trees would clear to her yard, I turned back. Repeated the same routine. Wrote her name. Carved another set of initials in another tree. Rehearsed the lines. Wrote 'Bobbie and Sandra' in the sand. Paddled to her house.

Nothing.

I couldn't just walk up to the house and knock on her back door. She needed to be in the back yard for the plan to work. I rowed back to Pirate's Island, the white shirt stuck to my back, soaked with sweat.

Okay. I took off the shirt and hung it on a tree. Swam in the river a bit. *Got to get the sweat off.* Cursed myself for failing to think of bringing deodorant. Put the shirt back on and once again headed to Sandra's house. I set my will. *If she's there, I will get out and talk to her.* I rowed slow and easy, but the sweat trickled down the center of my back.

As I rowed closer to her house, I could hear her muffled voice. Then I heard the most beautiful sound—her lilting laugh as it skipped across the water. I moved the oars like a whisper through the water to savor the moment and conserve sweat. She spoke again, her voice low. Swiveling my head to find her, I saw her sitting on the dock, just a few feet away.

With Andy Workman, a football player.

What to do? I floated into their view, rowing upstream. Turning now would look idiotic, so I rowed onward, and they came into full view, seated side by side on the dock with their feet in the water, holding hands. Sandra smiled and waved at me. I stopped rowing with one hand and waved back, then fumbled for the oar. It popped out of the oarlock and I lunged for it. The boat tipped and I shot over the gunwale and into the water. Sandra and Andy got a good laugh out of that. I climbed back into the boat and realized I failed to recover the oar. I rowed with the one oar like a paddle, as they said something. Mortified, I didn't hear what they said, except the word, 'Bobbie.' It sounded like a baby's name, not Bob, or Rob, or Robert or something. I caught up to the oar and leaned over to grab it. Please, don't fall in again. The boat turned toward the shore, so I rowed hard to straighten it.

No way was I going back by her yard. I bore down on the left oar and made a long arcing turn through the middle of the river, and soon, I could see the two of them on the dock.

Then Andy kissed her. Right on the mouth. I saw him do it. Then he pulled away and smiled at me, with a look that said, 'I got her. You don't.'

He may as well have stabbed me in the heart.

I rowed back home, a song in my head.

I had a girl
And Donna was her name.
Since she left me
I've never been the same.
Cause I love my girl
Donna, where can you be?

I stopped at Pirate's Island and carved the initials out of the trees, making it unreadable. Swept my feet over the names carved in the sand. Wadded up the shirt and threw it in the river. As it moved downstream and settled into the depths, I realized my mother would kill me when she found out I lost it.

I rowed home.

Crenshaw didn't seem to be around, so I swam a bit to cool off, the sun now bearing down and the humid air still as death. Wandering home, I stole from place to place, surveying the neighborhood to avoid Johnny Ray and his wrath. Mom met me at the kitchen and gave me a glass of lemonade, dripping with cold droplets on the glass. She had the radio on, and I sat on the couch with my feet on the coffee table. Perry Como sang. After his song, the announcer said, "And now, the Poni Tails." No, please. Not this song. Numerous women harmonized and stabbed my heart with the words.

> Born too late for you to notice me
> To you, I'm just a kid that you won't date
> Why was I born too late?

Mom walked in and said, "Are you okay, honey?"

I wiped my eyes and nodded. "This is a sad song."

"It sure is." She sat beside me, and I leaned into her. "You want to talk about it?"

I shook my head and stood. "Think I'll go find Johnny Ray. Head out to the river." I walked out of the room as the Poni Tails continued their assault.

> I see you walk with another
> I wish it could be me
> I long to hold and kiss you
> But know it never can be.

We'll go upriver and play trucks, pirates, Huck and Tom games. Do some fishing and fry them up. Maybe, Johnny Ray can pump his legs, let go of the rope swing today.

But I'll never go by Sandra's house again.

NANCY SANSONE

Nancy Sansone earned a Casino Management degree from College of Southern Nevada and studied creative writing at the University of Nevada, Las Vegas. Based on her twenty years' experience as a supervisor in the gaming industry, she created a fast-paced suspense thriller set in Las Vegas titled, *Calling Her Name*. She is currently working on the sequel.

Nancy is co-editor and co-coordinator of two books of biographical profiles of Nevada women in history, (Stephens Press, 2006 and 2013). Her short stories were published in *Writer's Bloc II* and *III* (Mystic Publishers, 2008 and 2010). She is an active member of the Henderson Writers' Group, Shared Words Writers' Group, several critique groups, and Southern Nevada Women's History Project. Nancy can be reached at www.nancysansoneauthor.com.

The Midnight Visitor

I arrived in Montello, Wisconsin all set for a weekend of nostalgia, but unprepared for what lay ahead. When my cousin Jane invited me to visit her new home, I never expected to travel back to the small town where our mothers grew up.

Jane met me at the door with a big grin. She reminded me of her mother, my Aunt Mary. "Come in, come in. I'm so excited you're here. Wait until you see what I've done."

The old house was elegant. I walked across the dark polished wood floor of the foyer and craned my neck to take in the sparkling Swarovski crystal chandelier hanging on a long, thick, gold chain twenty feet above us. Rooms on the first floor promised hours of investigation. Ahead, a beautiful oak staircase led up to the second floor.

"Well, what do you think?"

"It's great! I'm speechless. When you said you bought a fixer-upper, I never dreamed it was our old family home."

"I wanted to surprise you. Did you notice the old quarry when you drove by? It's really beautiful considering our great-great grandpa died there"

"It was too dark to see much, but it looked like a huge waterfall."

"After so many workers died in cave-ins, the town voted to close it and voila—it's a waterfall. We'll walk over tomorrow. But first, I can't wait to show you around my palace." She laughed with delight. "This place always fascinated me because it's over a hundred-years-old."

We spent the next hour going through the house, rooms rich in family history.

"Have you found any books or papers to help our genealogy search?" I asked.

"I put every paper and picture I could find in boxes. We can go through them tomorrow."

We agreed to change into our bedtime clothes and meet back in the library to relax in new soft cream colored leather chairs.

We drank wine, munched on cheese and crackers, and speculated about the discoveries we'd make.

I yawned. "I hate to poop out on you so early, but I'm exhausted...long drive and long day."

Jane sighed in reply. "I'm ready to go up, too. I'll be right down the hall in the large bedroom where Grandma and Grandpa slept. I've put you in the green bedroom. It must have been Aunt Jenny's, I mean your mom's, when she was young. With her bright red hair, green was probably her favorite color.

"You're right. Mom would have loved it. Maybe, I'll dream of her." I was excited so hurried upstairs to my room.

I threw my robe on the rocker and curled up under the green paisley comforter. I felt safe and certain it had been Mom's room. A silly thought came to me when I sniffed. I could swear I smelled Mom's Elizabeth Arden dusting powder.

During the night, someone touched me on the shoulder, just lightly, but enough to alarm me. I woke up with a start. "Jane?" No answer. I rolled onto my side, and then abruptly sat up and turned on the lamp on the nightstand. I almost screamed at the sight of an old woman sitting in the rocker at the foot of my bed. My first instinct was to race out of the room, but I leaned in for a closer look. Grandma! This was impossible. She died over forty years ago and would now be a hundred plus many years, but she looked the same as she had in my childhood.

Now, I was scared. Had I died in this old house? Did Grandma come to welcome me to the other side? If I run away, will I live? She reached out and took my hand. Hers was warm and surprisingly, I immediately felt at peace and let her lea,d me out of the room.

In the hallway, we entered a door I hadn't noticed earlier. The stairs going up were dusty and creaked with each footstep. At the top, we reached a second door. I opened it and turned to ask Grandma where we were, but she had disappeared. Light from the moon filtered through a small window and welcomed me inside.

I moved further in and to my surprise found myself in my childhood bedroom with all of my treasures in pristine condition. My roller skates leaned against the dresser I'd shared with my sisters. Several paper-doll books lay on a table where I'd spent hours cutting out dolls and their clothes. The wicker rocking chair in the corner of the room looked like the same one my grandpa used to rock me in. I laughed aloud when I spotted my precious Annie McGuffy doll. Her brown hair was done in neat braids just like I wore as a child. Mom told me we were almost twins, hazel eyes and all.

I sensed company in the room and turned expecting to catch Grandma watching. I gasped and tears filled my eyes. It wasn't her. It was my mom! Jenny! Reaching for her, she pulled me to her. The scent of Evening in Paris perfume enveloped me. I remembered being intrigued by the dark blue bottle with the name written in cursive sitting on her vanity. The years evaporated immediately and I was a little girl again held, in the safety of my mother's arms.

She spoke softly, "You always wanted to be a writer, now have faith in yourself."

"What do you mean?" I asked. "Do you know that I lost my self-confidence when my husband died? Do you know how much I'm struggling with my writing?"

Mom smiled and kissed me on the cheek, then she turned and disappeared.

In the morning, I woke up in the green bedroom with the paisley comforter wrapped tight around me. I stretched, feeling rested and at peace. The enticing smell of morning coffee drifted into my room through the heating vent. My dream had been wonderful. I couldn't wait to tell Jane about it. What I saw when I picked up my robe from the rocker, made me lightheaded, and I nearly fainted.

My Annie McGuffy doll sat waiting for me.

LAUREN TALLMAN

Currently a resident of Las Vegas, NV, author Lauren Tallman was born in Lithuania. Raised in New York, wanderlust led her to Israel for most of her life. After working with hi-tech billion dollar company CEOs, she moved back to the States. Her first book, *How To Have An Affair and Not Get Caught*, reached #1 on Amazon. She is currently preparing *The Erotic Tales of Renni* for publication. Lauren's skilled writing extends to the comical, the heart-warming, and the romantic. A number of her short stories have been published in anthologies. Her works have been mentioned by Robin Leach, as well as in Las Vegas' *CityLife*.

Lightning

Let them run. Don't follow.

All across the park people grabbed children and blankets, dogs and drinks, and made the mad dash to cars that stood too far away. As a family rushed past, their little girl looked at me, eyes wide, hand held high.

"Lady, rain!" the little girl yelled, pointing to the black clouds rumbling behind me. Her feet barely touched the grass as her mother pulled her along.

No. I will sit here.

The trees around me stood straight, waiting for the downpour. I stared at the memorial plaque set on the ground before a tall sapling.

"David Herald — September 1, 2013"

I crossed my arms and legs and watched the lake tremble. The mass of fowl hurried to their little island and huddled together for shelter.

Remember how you convinced me to swim naked in the sea? We dipped into the clear green water. The sunlight streaked down and I swirled the water and light with my fingers. Little fish came to watch us, unafraid, but darting when we kicked our legs. Oh, your long legs. The muscles rippled as you swam past me, and I put my hand out to touch them. You pressed your hands over my ribs. I thought you would touch my breasts. You gave a mighty kick and we flew up to the surface, gasping and coughing, gulping air, laughing, but you did not let go, and then you touched them.

Drops, the size of quarters, thumped onto the bench, more and more followed. Torrents of rain crashed down and

117

my hair stuck to my forehead and cheeks. My lips hurt from pressing them together, my eyes burned from lack of tears.

"Hey lady, you ok?"

A young man, tall like my David, stared as he pulled his shirt over his head against the storm. I nodded and looked away. He hesitated, bouncing from one foot to the other. Lightning crashed and he ran off.

Another David lost.

Drops smacked down leaves that, before, had rolled along.

We have been slapped down, haven't we, David? The gods have played with us. You kissed me that morning. Your arms wrapped around me. Looking out to the mountains, your chin pressing onto my head, making me laugh. I leaned into your hard body and was warm. When I looked up, you said "Kiss me," and I did.

My head whirled. The winds cut into my skin through my blouse. I stood, arms out, alone with the strongest of elements, head held high, drops pouring onto my closed eyes in place of tears that refused to come. Clouds collided, the thunder deafening. I walked onto the open area, slipping along on the silky grass.

"David! Daaaaviiiid!"

Blinding lightning slicked thru the sky.

David! Do it.

My chest heaved. I smiled madly and watched as a flash came toward me in slow motion, burning my eyes. I closed them and waited. In a second, searing heat shot into the ground at my feet. I flew back, head banging on the ridge of the bench, elbows stinging from the graze, back hurting from the impact. I heard nothing but my heavy breaths and wild heartbeat in my ears. I sat up. The black hole in the earth was filling from the deluge.

And then it stopped. It just stopped. The rain, the winds, the thunder, all gone, and I was still here.

Hands trembling, I checked my elbows for scrapes, pressed my lower back against the pain. I got up, brushed leaves from my behind and looked around. The gleaming white ducks left their cluster and entered the sparkling water, shaking their heads and flapping their wings. Shining tree limbs dipped with the heavy weight of drops propelling to the ground. Even the sun popped out from behind random ivory clouds. I had to smile.

Washed clean, eh, David?

I walked out of the park. At the curb cars splashed by, water shooting out in perfect arcs from under the wheels. My shoes squished on the pavement as I went home.

I peeled off my clothes, shook my head, and laughed when drops hit the mirror in perfectly aligned streaks. I put on his flannel sweats and they brushed softly on my naked body. The shirt was so large I had to fold it around me to keep the cool air from rushing in underneath. I lay on the couch with knees bent, my feet crushing the cushions for warmth. Drying wisps of hair tickled my forehead and cheeks. They made me shudder, but I did not move them. My hands tucked into the folds of the shirt, pulling it down, and I felt my breath sweep into the neckline and warm my breasts.

Do you remember lying like this, David? Me, too.

And I slept.

WILLIAM F. WALLES

Bill Walles writes mainstream novels pairing well-developed characters with dynamic plots. He believes fiction nears the truth when individuals scramble from the pressures that crush lives. Bill endured forty years of non-profit management and an unsuccessful entrepreneurial career launched during the Great Recession. A semi-tired resident of Henderson, NV, he attends the Henderson Writers' Group, freelances, edits, and coaches writers. His novel, *All About the Money*, will be published in 2014.

Mansion in the Sky

The white stucco glowed. Standing across the narrow street from the bungalow, he looked down the hill and watched the ocean waves run, one following another onto the pink sand beach. The breeze climbing the embankment mixed ocean salt with tropical florals.

Like a brochure he had seen, he was sure of it.

"Cameron. Cameron, over here," the baritone voice yelled.

From the side of the house, a man strode toward him, the face familiar, the name escaping him. He wore resort casual, a light-weight polo with What's-his-name's logo over the heart. Why was he having trouble remembering?

"You look so much better than when I last saw you," the man said.

Cameron looked down. His pants, the right inside seam ripped from crotch to cuff, stuck to the leg, the fabric sooted black, the visible portion of the thigh rippled with burned skin, coagulated splashed blood from a wound an inch or so to the side of his exposed penis. His balance dropped faster than his blood pressure, the ground began to swirl.

He looked at the man two feet in front, the smile calm and ... reassuring? Cameron glanced at his arm, the lower portion hanging, attached to the elbow only by a tendon and fried skin.

"Don't worry, you'll be fine before we get in the house." The stranger turned and walked toward the side of the cottage.

The blue eyes—more than familiar. The hair hung longer in the back.

"Jesus?"

His host stopped, looked over his shoulder, and nodded.

"O my Lord." Cameron dropped to his knees, a move that hurt very little. He clasped his hands, the right arm already re-attached and the burnt skin reforming as he watched.

"Since everyone knows me here, I ask them to call me Jay."

Jay? Something was wrong. The Escalade came from the left corner of his vision as he turned onto S. Eastern. They had eaten with Paul and Tina's family. Barbeque. Dead.

He stared at Jesus.

"That's right, you still expect that unending worship and bowing. We interpret that differently than you do. Heaven is a place to rejoice and give thanks, but in the arena of a new and resurrected community." Jesus stretched a hand and swept it at the horizon.

"Quiet today. We always give the newly arrived a few days—or whatever they need to adjust. Love. Joy. Healing. Your body is the first step."

Cameron felt for the pants leg. The rip gone, he felt no pain. His gaze riveted, he watched the fabric brighten and the last stains fade. The smell of ash, which he accepted as normal, disappeared and transformed into bluff floral.

He had driven with Chris and Conner. The accident.

"They're not here, Cameron."

They're in…

"No, they're not in hell. The accident only happended four minutes ago. They'll be in ambulances in another two or three minutes and taken to emergency. You know how good Dr. Tanaka is. Relax. You took the brunt of the damage. T-boned, right behind your seat."

That fucking bastard.

"Yeah, he was going seventy trying to beat the yellow light." Jesus shook his head. "I'm sorry. I read minds. I shouldn't, especially when people first arrive. I'll stop and let you have some privacy. You ask what you want, when you want."

Jay held the waist high decorative gate open for Cameron. The back yard stretched for acres, the grass even in every direction.

What else would he expect?

"You've got more questions than you can manage. Everyone does," Jay chuckled. "Not that your concerns aren't important. It's that in a short time, you'll find that earthly stuff, things you never figured out, get answered and put aside or you find a different perspective. Now, it's kinda tough. Huh?"

"Who was he?"

"Mr. Seventy-mile-per-hour? Carl Santiago."

"Carl! My golf buddy?"

"Wasn't his car. His wife's. He stayed a little late at a private party and was rushing to get home before his wife returned from the girls' monthly soiree."

"Bastard. Steaming pile of…"

"Yeah, sad." Jay clapped Cameron on the shoulder. "You hungry? Everyone seems to be ravenous when they get here. Something about the transfer from 'one plane of existence to another.'"

The den inside the slider had a nine foot leather couch fronted by a low table filled with skewers of chicken and beef, platters of vegetables, chips and dips, cold beer in a barrel of ice, fruit—well, everything Cameron ever wanted.

"Sit. Enjoy. Body healing is one thing. Leaving the cobwebs behind, that takes longer."

They sat and talked. One question opened to a clear and satisfying answer. Another question followed. Another perfect answer.

In time, Cameron relaxed. Jay, um, Jesus, explained the universe and so many biting points of confusion. But nothing personal. Cameron couldn't approach the things of his heart. He was afraid to ask about…

"Hey," Jay said. "Just in time. It's the best part of the week. Yeah, we still have weeks here. The old Sabbath thing, every seventh day. You'll get the hang of it."

On the far side of the food table, the floor retracted against the wall.

Cameron expected a television. Stupid. Heaven wouldn't rely on clumsy technology. And Jesus wouldn't be locked into some bundled cable or satellite dish package.

A crowd scene appeared. Perfectly clear, the 3-D effect boggling. And the people started screaming—with fear. What?

"It's not technology, at all. We get visions of the real thing."

"What…is this?"

"Boiled in Oil Thursday, by far the most exciting day of the week." Jay adjusted himself on the couch, slipping off his sandals and sliding his bare feet onto the table, his white skin gleaming, his toe nails perfectly cut.

"Boiled in Oil?"

"Life here gets to be monotonous, let's be real. No arguments. All those old, unsingable hymns. No rain. You know." Jay offered that rich smile. "So, we check on Hell. We all know many of the residents. They can see us and be reminded what they could have had. And we get a little excitement."

Excitement? People in Heaven need excitement? Jay, Jesus needs excitement?

"Okay, here we go. Twenty-four hours of chaos."

A face stared directly at Cameron. "Is that Carl?"

"Sure is. Guess he didn't last in the ambulance."

The sixty-year-old roared with pain as a shower of what smelled like bacon grease splashed over the philandering speeder's back. The skin erupted with boils and burns. The agony knocked him to the ground where Carl struggled to find a footing. When he found purchase, the former CEO dashed for a crevice in the red rock.

"Ooh, he's getting it now." Jay reached for a chicken drumstick. "After the day is over, they forget the whole experience so that each Thursday the excitement and the knowledge that there is no escape is fresh, new, and terrifying."

Screams splashed against the bungalow walls as one cascade of fiery oil followed another onto hysterical, defenseless figures.

Carl's face exploded in flame as darker oil combusted with skin and hair.

"I don't want to watch this," Cameron said.

"Wait now, you believe in Hell. Your pastor has been very clear. Accept me, you come here. Sin or don't believe and you get the wages. What did you expect Hell to be?" Jay shifted, leaning forward. "Zowie, that one hurt."

Those who could look upward saw Him and cried in their pain. "Jesus, save us."

"That's the part I hate. They had a shot, each of them."

Cameron heard his name. On the second shout, he located the woman. Maddie!

"You didn't know she was lesbian?"

He couldn't look at either Carl or Maddie. He saw a child limp into view.

"Reformed Jew, just bar mitzvahed. Not even orthodox."

"Dad, Dad."

God. God Almighty, stop this.

"Neither of them made it. Tanaka does good work, but he can't perform miracles."

"You can." Cameron felt the anger. "You said they weren't going to hell."

The smile had faded. "I said they were being taken to the hospital."

"They don't deserve to be in Hell, not with those people. They're…"

"Sinners, Cameron. Sinners. Chris didn't have the same, pure faith as you. Conner asked too many questions, already. Not everyone gets to enter Heaven."

"Let me take their place, Lord."

"Cameron, you know the rules."

"It's not right. They don't belong there."

Jay sat, His mouth in a pout.

Cameron pleaded. "No one deserves that. If they can't come here, let me go there to be with them."

The smile returned.

"Okay, people, that's a wrap. He gets it."

WILLIAM DARRAH WHITAKER

Darrah Whitaker is a graduate of the University of Virginia with a B.A. in Foreign Affairs and holds two Master degrees (MA-Film/MBA) from the University of Texas. He has written five screenplays, one which was produced and another optioned. His short stories, "My Life as a Sperm" and "Diary of a Delusional Reunionist" were published in the *Writers Bloc III* and *IV* anthologies. He is an active member of the International Thriller Writers and also a member of the Henderson Writers' Group in Las Vegas, Nevada, serving as Conference Coordinator on the Board of Directors. His first novel, *The Santiago Agenda*, which is due out this Spring, 2014, incorporates elements of Darrah's experiences and is inspired by his grandfather's work with the Office of Strategic Services (OSS), the precursor to the CIA.

A Shadow Always

The shadow stained the corner of the room. It didn't fade away like it sometimes did.

Tonight it stayed, motionless.

But not indifferent. I knew that.

Defective neon buzzed like angry bees through my open window. Desperate flashes danced around the room, but not into the corner where the shadow lurked. I watched and waited for it to move until my eyes began to tear.

Still, it remained, patient.

I gave up and tried to fall back asleep, back into my dream where I was happy.

There, I watched my wife play with our children on the swings in our backyard where the large oak provided comforting shade. Hamburgers sizzled over hot coals, and I felt tiny pricks jump onto my skin as I turned them one last time. I was about to call out when something tore me from my dream.

Now, it was too late.

The shadow in the corner moved…or, maybe, it was a trick.

"What do you want?" I said.

I knew it wasn't real. It couldn't be. I knew it wouldn't answer. It never did.

The shadow thrived here in my single, sad room with the rusted bed that folded into the wall, my room with the unforgiving floor that creaked with age and weakness, my room with neighbors who screamed late into the night. I paid the man downstairs each week for the privilege of staying here. Each week I resolved to leave and, each week, I paid him again.

"Tell me what you want."

It said nothing in return, but I already knew.

Chill night air invaded the room. I drew my blanket close and turned away.

Slowly, curiosity compelled me to look again…into the corner…into the darkness of the shadow.

He still stood there; watched me. No longer a thing. It was a man now, with empty, soulless eyes.

I pulled my feet close to my body and stared back.

"I don't want to do this anymore."

Had I negotiated with him before?

"What's the game tonight?" I yelled.

I remembered. We'd played it many times before. There would be no bargaining. The game was simple. Only one rule.

I lose.

"I have to make it to morning," I told him. "I can do that."

That's right. I'd done it before.

If I made it to morning, I would survive. That was the game I played. If I could survive, if I could withstand the chill, if I could make it to the light, I'd win.

"I can beat you."

Did he laugh? Maybe. I would show him.

Tomorrow, I would wander the streets until I found a park where I could sit and enjoy the sun; feel its warmth bathe me as it once had. I'd dream again, free of the room and its shadow. Nothing to tear me away from my children's easy laughter, the caress of my wife's arms reaching around my waist and pulling me close, the cool touch of the wind on my face, all the simple pleasures.

He laughed again, and I knew why.

Making it to the morning wasn't winning. It simply meant more of the same. He made sure of that.

I should have left a long time ago. I should have left the day I arrived, but by then, it was too late. I stayed to fight alone with the shadow man in the corner.

I slid my arm under the sheets toward the floor and felt for the metal pipe kept there for protection. My fingers brushed it and it rolled away on the hard wood. I glanced to the corner. The shadow had moved closer while I wasn't watching. He moved closer, sensing what I planned to do. He moved closer to stop me.

I shot up in bed and screamed like my neighbors screamed. "Get the fuck out of here."

I dove for the floor to find the pipe before the shadow man found me. I would smash it over and over into his shadow head until nothing was left.

He pounced, dragging me down even more. I tried to break free. He straddled my body. His weight drove precious breath from me, crushed my strength, extinguished my will. He dug hypodermic claws into my arm, tore into my flesh, deep and satisfying, and I knew I could not escape.

He lowered his face to mine and grinned at me, a wicked, unrelenting smile that promised everything and nothing. His hot breath soured the air. I smelled his decay, and nausea swept over me. A growl emerged from his gaping hole that shifted into that slow, mocking laugh, taunting me for all I had lost.

I couldn't let him win. Not again. My free hand groped for the weapon. Then I felt cold steel. For a brief moment, I had hope. I grasped the pipe and struck out blindly. I felt the impact, heard the thud of metal against something soft and giving.

I scrambled up and swayed on unsteady legs. My hand trembled and the pipe fell to the floor.

The shadow lay there, motionless, but not indifferent.

I knew that.

I waited. Finally, it moved.

A dark patch spilled from its head and floated across the floor toward me. I stepped back as it spread.

The shadow had taken everything from me, but it still wanted more.

My only salvation was the light. All I had to do was cross the room and turn on the light.

It reached out.

I didn't move. I didn't turn on the light. The thing thrived in the darkness, from the pain and misery found there, the place where I lived, and yet I didn't move.

I did nothing except wait.

I wanted it to touch me. I had done this before. I had looked at the shadow and, each time, I let it consume me and draw me back into the abyss.

I didn't want the light.

I didn't want to see.

I wanted only darkness.

TEASERS
(Excerpts from Novels)

A.L. CAMPBELL

A.L. Campbell hand-scribed her first novel, a time-travel romance, at age fourteen, and then put aside writing for a career in the U.S. Air Force. The writing bug chomped again following retirement, resulting in the storyline for a five-book YA/SciFi series, the AJ Silver *Mis*Adventures, set in the future. "Exposed" is a teaser for *The Gift of Ancestors*, the first book of the series. She also writes short stories to round out the world of AJ Silver. "The Selection" and "Waterheart" appear in *Writers Bloc III* and *IV*, respectively. "The Round-Up" can be found in the anthology *A World of Their Own* by Nightfall Publications. A.L. attends Nevada State College in pursuit of a Visual Media degree and serves as Secretary for the Henderson Writers' Group, hosts of the Las Vegas Writer's Conference.

Exposed

AJ wished she could be anywhere other than sitting among all the other eighth graders in the school's multipurpose room. The outward quiet of her fellow test-takers contradicted their inner thoughts—thoughts that she couldn't shut out.

"…like best…"

"…music, I like music…"

"…lead or follow?"

"…stupid questions…"

She'd hoped to take the DCP, the once-in-a-lifetime career placement exam that would determine the course of the rest of her life, in homeroom like the normal end-of-year tests just for this reason—people couldn't keep their thoughts to themselves. Even though she was used to hearing random thoughts, the forced proximity of so many people strained her sanity. Thankfully, almost everyone focused on the questions before them.

Can they even be called questions?

After an opportunity to list any career she might be interested in—which she'd passed up—the words in the holograph had repeated over and over in her head as her classmates read them: lists of activities to mark likes or dislikes, followed by random statements to agree or disagree with.

Taking her time, she shoved intruding thoughts to the back of her head and tried to focus on her answers, one question at a time.

"You bitch! …knew I liked him…"

The disjointed thought pierced AJ's skull with a viciousness that blurred her vision and soured the lunch in her stomach. Her head snapped up and her eyes scanned the direction it came from.

Positioned alphabetically at the long tables, everyone faced the same direction. Her gaze swept over the backs of heads, searching for blond tresses. This voice she recognized. Becka Johnson's acid tones sounded the same in thought as they did out loud. Several rows forward on the right, she'd twisted in her chair to face the back.

AJ's heart jumped. *What did I do?* Seconds later, she suspected Becka's attention extended beyond her and peered over her left shoulder.

At the rear of the room, in the direct line of fire, sat Daphne West. Becka's usual best friend fluttered her lashes at the popular boy seated next to her.

Intent on the projected image before him, Pete Warren didn't notice her antics.

Daphne turned her head in Becka's—and AJ's—direction a second before donning a too-late-to-be-believed innocent facade. *"What? ...he's so dap...he likes me..."*

He didn't look that good to AJ—pretty is as pretty does, she remembered from somewhere—and she'd heard enough of his thoughts to consider "dappy" a better description for such a fake.

Catching AJ watching, Daphne thought, *"Freak!"*

Whatever. I've heard worse. The name-calling didn't bother AJ, but she pivoted back to her table.

"...asks me first, he's mine," Daphne silently declared.

"Back-stabber...know how much I like Pete..."

Great! Just what I need—a silent fight that's only going to hurt me, and I can't get up and leave. AJ strove to ignore them.

Other classmates finished. Their thoughts once again wandered and mingled with Becka's hostility.

A terrible pressure throbbed in AJ's right temple. Rubbing the spot, she closed both eyes—and heard Pete's thoughts shift.

"…looking at me…you're friends…"

AJ felt his excitement and amusement.

"Come here…secret."

Becka's anger flared. *"Get away from him! He's mine!"*

Pete basked in the tension — the power their attentiveness gave him.

Clothes rustled next to AJ and she opened her eyes. An empty seat away, her younger brother, Quinn, got up and took his keypad without glancing her way. Boy Wonder had finished, completely unaware of the drama playing out in the minds around them. At least, it seemed that way to her. She didn't know for sure since, for some unknown reason, she never heard *his* thoughts.

She forced her attention back to the floating words and struggled to understand them. *What was I doing?* The words made no sense. *I have to get out of here. Answer the questions. Finish and get out.*

With pain blurring her vision, she marked the remaining answers indiscriminately.

Done.

Grabbing the thin, flexible keypad, she rose and walked down her row to the side of the room. A watery glance showed her that a line had formed. She rushed to the end. Blinking to clear her sight, she looked forward. Daphne stood two people ahead.

"Bitch! …wait 'til we get outside…"

Becka's words speared her skull from behind, trapping AJ between them once more.

Thoughts flew from all directions, but Becka's overpowered the others.

AJ's temples pounded. The chaos overwhelmed her. Pressure built. If it didn't ease soon, she'd pop.

Then, something took over — a survival instinct or something. Without thinking, AJ rounded on Becka. "Stop it! You and Daphne are making me sick! You're supposed to be best friends and you're fighting over a boy that doesn't like either of you! He just wants to see you fight over him!"

She whipped around to face Daphne. "So, stop it!"

The world silenced—even in her head.

Panning the stunned faces, AJ found all eyes fixed on her. *What have I done?* Her heart raced. Heat flooded her face. *Get out. Get out.*

The order took control of her body, urging her past the ogling faces in line to the testers. Cutting in front, she handed over the pad with a mumbled "sorry" and headed for the entrance.

Quinn stood just outside the open doors with his friends. He laughed as she passed him. "Way to go, AJ."

Her clipped "shut up" earned another laugh.

AJ ran to the courtyard, where'd she'd promised to meet Cassie. Finding it empty and not seeing her friend, she sat on a corner bench with her knees pulled up tight. Her forehead met her legs, causing her braid to swing to the side.

Alexandra Jai Silver, she imagined her mother's scolding voice, *what have you done?*

How could she possibly explain what had happened? *Lost control—that's what. This is so not good. How can I fix this?* Her jumbled mind came up with no solution.

Only Cassie knew that she heard things—her family didn't. She'd tried to tell her mother once, back in kindergarten. No one had believed her. That's when she understood she was different. Before then, she'd been happy and normal. A sour taste rose at the back of her throat as she realized *that* scene had involved Becka Johnson, too.

Becka, outspoken even then, and a dark-haired boy had shared a game table with her. AJ had wanted to make friends. The boy played with some toy she remembered liking. Becka must have, too, because she'd watched and silently referred to him as Raghead.

When he'd put down the toy, AJ had asked, "Can I play with that, Raghead?" She hadn't known any better.

The teacher had sputtered, unable to speak. Becka had stared at her like she had two heads. The boy had looked ready to cry.

AJ didn't understand then what had happened. Her mom, who worked on the League flagship, had been home at the time. As much as AJ had insisted that Becka had called the boy by that name, the teacher had denied it. No one had believed her. She'd never forgotten.

The boy, whose real name she couldn't recall, left. Becka never became her friend. Instead, she'd bad-mouthed AJ to the other kids. If for no other reason, they stayed away from her in fear that Becka would talk about them the same way.

No loss there. Becka treated her friends just as bad. Although more playmates when she was younger would've been nice, in hindsight, AJ convinced herself she'd learned more *because* they kept their distance. Then, in fourth grade, she met Cassie before anyone could warn her off, and they'd been best friends ever since.

Shuffled footsteps drew AJ's head up. She shook her head before Cassie could say anything. Wordlessly, they left school.

Clusters of students stared as they passed. Their overheard stage whispers matched what they thought — that AJ had finally lost it.

The occasional hover transport passed near them, probably taking a student home.

They reached a business area, away from the school crowds, before Cassie busted out laughing.

Is crazy contagious? AJ stopped and stared at her lunatic friend.

Between gasps of laughter, Cassie asked, "Did you see their faces?" Unable to contain herself, she doubled over.

"Yes, I saw them. I..." AJ recalled the image of dumbstruck faces staring at her. *They* were *comical.* The longer she considered it, the funnier it seemed, until a near hysterical bark erupted from her throat.

The sound set off a new round of laughter in them both. Tears streamed down their faces. AJ's headache finally eased.

They pulled themselves together with effort and

resumed walking, but took turns acting out the shocked expressions. Each time they collapsed in bellows of laughter all over again.

The humor diminished to occasional giggles by the time they spotted the group ahead of them.

BOBBI BOLAND WHITE

Bobbi White grew up in the coal mining district of Lackawanna County, Pennsylvania, surrounded by dogs, horses, and stories of mine collapse tragedies. (Her current fictional trilogy concerns the abandoned mines of central Nevada.) Bobbi went to Catholic school, graduated from the University of Pennsylvania with a "Most Creative Student" award, and began teaching at-risk teens. She spent seven years in the Caribbean, continued teaching troubled youth in Miami, married, raised four children, taught in California, lived in Vancouver, Canada, directed a vocational school in Las Vegas, and worked as managing editor of the Las Vegas Peoples Press. She has won several awards for her writing, including the Montaigne Medal for her published novel, *Escape From Marianna*. Bobbi is a peace activist, an animal and environmental advocate, and is happiest when she is "on the road again."

Tobias

Tobias had survived Death Valley but the journey had taken a terrible toll. The pads on his feet were torn as he limped slowly among the miles of deserted mines, their boarded entrances crumbling into broken pieces, no longer needed to keep thieves away, no longer good for anything – like him. Tobias closed his eyes, pressed back in the dark cave of an abandoned mine, hungry, exhausted, alone.

That winter Tobias experienced a hunger that his heart had never known, a terrible emptiness. Every dawn, he would lie at the mouth of his lonely cave, and he would study the coyotes that loped silently through the early light below. They were so much like him—the way they moved. The silent way they paused and turned to look at him. They also were lonely. They also suffered. And even when he never saw them, he could hear them and it was enough. He could hear their prayers, their calling out across the night, across the low clouds, across the lifespan of a planet that had known them for a million years. Their prayers seemed familiar to Tobias—like a song, so that he drew comfort from them. And he would often fall asleep to this song.

He longed to meet one of them, touch one of them. However, they mostly traveled in twos or threes, slowing briefly to acknowledge him, then moving on. It was not until the winter's coldest days, stark and desolate, that he noticed a change. Now, as he walked slowly through the rocky land, down into the dry canyons looking for a trickle of water, a morsel of food, the few coyotes that he passed seemed more docile than before, giving him a wider birth, more respectful of his chosen path.

He was taller than most of them, yet much thinner. Perhaps, they could tell that he was getting old, a sad cousin on the same brief path as theirs through life, his coat hanging loosely on bones that were swollen, brittle, near starvation but proudly enduring his hunger, at home on the brown land, privileged to have had his few Springs, learned his few lessons, beaten down by loneliness, ravaged by the elements but still not ready to succumb.

And then one dawn, a female came to him. She looked silently at Tobias, appearing at the edge of his cave, her golden eyes clear and questioning. He had no idea what to do, and so he stood and took one step toward her and stopped. She cautiously began to circle him, slowly moving ever closer while he stayed rigid and still, trembling slightly but not understanding why he trembled. And then, carefully, she touched him, laid her head lightly on his back, breathing gently into his fur. Tobias could feel her heartbeat; that's how close to him she stood. He turned his head to her ever so slightly and then she did the most amazing thing: she looked up at him and gave him her breath completely. It was clean and fresh—a sweetness that dove within him to a place he could not name, had never experienced.

She backed up quickly then, and just before she disappeared, she paused, the sky a cobalt blue behind her. And it seemed to Tobias that she smiled at him, that her eyes smiled. Maybe, she did. Or, maybe not. It was a look, however, that she wrote on his heart, and he would treasure it throughout his life, and even beyond it.

He dreamed of her that night, dreamed that she had come again to him, and lay against him. And when he awoke he still sensed her, and he pawed at the dirt where she had lain in his dream, and he could feel her all about him.

But she was gone, and a great emptiness opened within Tobias, and he felt that he could not go on. He had obeyed the angel. He had done his best. But for Tobias, the end still loomed. Weariness had halted his journey, pressed in upon him dulling his eyes, weighing his shoulders low to the ground. And every muscle ached. And his heart within him ached.

Tobias experienced only one human contact that winter in the brown hills, moving slowly from the shelter of one abandoned mine to the next, but it was a welcome one and it reminded him of the young girl who had found him in some weeds beside the road where someone had thrown him—thrown him away, when he was new.

She had taken such tender care of him, stroking his fur and giving him milk and small bits of food from her hand. She had played with him, taken him on long walks, and promised she would never leave him.

But she must have forgotten that promise, because one day she took him to a long yard that reached all the way to the sea where he was expected to guard the property of humans whom he did not know, humans who did not love him. She had told him that he must be good and wait for her. "Stay. Toby," she had told him. "Stay."

So Tobias stayed.

But the yard was a lonely place for Tobias, and once he discovered several hidden spots along the fence where he could dig unnoticed, he would tunnel out to look for her. Month after month he had ranged across the land, traveling up and down the country roads searching...searching... always for her. Where was she? Where had she gone? Crushed with failure, each time he would return to the yard, and crawl back under the fence. Perhaps, if he stayed there long enough, she would come back for him. But she never did.

And then, after years of waiting and of loneliness, even these who did not love him abandoned him. He saw them go, watched the moving trucks go down the driveway in a line. At first he thought they would return. He paced. He checked his food and water bowls. Finally, he just gave up.

He lay down by the gate one final time, and closed his eyes. Until the angel came.

So now, when Tobias looked down from his cave one morning and saw the human walking alone, shouldering a backpack, investigating the nooks and crannies below him, his feelings were mixed. Perhaps, this stranger was cruel. He was a man, and Tobias knew that men in the wild were often predators. But the need in the heart of Tobias outweighed his fears and outweighed his weariness, and against all survival instincts he threw caution to the wind and bounded down the rocks, wagging his tale furiously.

The stranger stopped. He smiled. And then he laughed heartily. "Well, 'ol fella, look at you! I bet you're thirsty—here…" and stooping down, the man made a cone out of some paper and poured fresh water into it. And Tobias drank. And drank. He would gladly have gone home with this man, given him his heart, stayed with him forever. But it was not to be.

The man stopped walking when Tobias began to follow him. He turned, directed Tobias to go from him. His whole demeanor changed, and Tobias could sense that the man was burdened with problems of his own and had no room in his life for another soul, another problem.

So his tail drooped. "Oh, don't worry," the man's voice gentled, "if I see you out here again, I'll have a piece of bread for you…maybe a sandwich."

So Tobias, who understood there was a sliver of hope that the man with the backpack would return, lay in his cave day after day and searched the trails below him. He had been nearing a town when he had stopped to make this cave his home, and on several occasions he had seen a truck on the rutted road to his south. But no one had come this close to him before, this close to *his* cave, to *his* mine.

It was several days before he saw the man with the backpack again, but this time he did not approach him. This time the man had a companion with him, and the companion had a rifle and walked with a purpose.

The accident that occurred that day, the sudden sound of panic from the men below, struck a deep fear into Tobias and sent him cowering back into his cave. When he emerged, his friend was gone and his friend's companion was running back to the road where he had left his truck. Tobias watched as the man ran. He remembered the voice of the man and the sound of his body as he walked below Tobias' cave. And Tobias kept these things in his mind.

When the man started his truck and drove away, Tobias crept down to the mine that the men had been exploring, and he found the shaft into which his friend had fallen. He listened but there was no sound from the depths of the narrow shaft. He whimpered; he pawed the dirt, circled, and pawed at it again. Finally, he lay down by the opening. This man had been a friend to him. He would keep watch.

Tobias did not move for several hours, until he heard the truck coming back. And then he fled.

2013 STUDENT WRITING CONTEST WINNERS

COLLEGE LEVEL

From Glyphs to Graffiti
Deuvall Dorsey

From historic stories and glorious fables
of notorious swordsmen seated at round tables
to futuristic time travelers from alternate dimensions
misplaced within our own present space and time continuum
times elusive attributes continuously constitute the center
    stage
when any pen or pencil dances on a page
from scribes of ancient days scribbling away
to intimately stroking keys upon a keyboard in the modern
    age.
Time is all encompassing combined with ever present,
past beyond the future with its origins amongst the essences,
once wedded with the written word disseminated lessons,
through letters to the future in a message from the past
as chapters from a book reveal the hour glass
And we turn the page to realize our times arrived at last.
Like obituaries of fire fighters in 1984
to all the ancient libraries that burn down in a war.
Stranded in a world where nothing is as it were before,
entire realms of worlds existing only in imagination
travel the planet intercontinentaly with captivating
    fascination.
As an eye being plucked from a socket whose only crime
    was that of reading
to literary masterpieces which are based upon deceiving.

Thoughts are constantly relayed from as far as millennia
    away
etched carved and engraved upon rocks and walls in all the
    glyphs that they display.
Well placed words written out wildly
outweighs the weight of words well written and strung
    together mildly.

HIGH SCHOOL LEVEL

The Lifestyle of Running
Kate Vanderstelt

Her breathing rate quickens as she increases her turnover. "You have 800 (meters) to go!" a coach yells. *800 meters to go,* she thought, *in my last race of the season. What am I going to do with it?* And with that, she loses all control. Brain dead, her legs take over, and before she knows it she crosses the finish line with a time of 22:05.7. That race was mine. And that girl is me.

For the longest time, running has been an adoration of mine. Ever since my older sister joined her high school Cross Country team I couldn't wait to reach the ninth grade and follow in her strides. I could only dream of the day my heart would be beating on the starting line as the gun was about to go off. For me, that day was August 28, 2012. Now, don't get me wrong; I had raced plenty of times before, but it had never been as serious as this for I had never run in a competitive high school race. On the day of the first race, I was so nervous; I couldn't concentrate in any of my six classes, because I was mulling over the fact that I would be racing in a few hours. I was worried I'd screw up and wouldn't race well. I wouldn't make varsity. *Varsity.* All I ever dreamed about while watching my sister race was being able to accomplish what she did: running on the varsity team all four years of her high school career. And now, after the countless weeks of formidable training and races, I have set myself up to achieve at the varsity level.

This season of Cross Country 2012, I was the only freshman on our team to run in the top seven, earning myself a varsity spot. But I won't be accepting this year's varsity letter for doing nothing. I won the Frosh-Soph race, which earned me the title of "fastest freshman in the city." I ran second on the team for two consecutive races. I ran away from every competition knowing that during the race I had given my all. I ran my way to the honor of being able to say I was The varsity. And if dedication and hard work doesn't show that I love my sport, I don't know what does.

Non-running friends of mine always ask, "How do you actually *like* to run?" My response, "You won't understand until you've experienced the thrill of racing," is typical. In fact, this statement is true. Practice itself is not enjoyable until the athlete knows the feeling of what she is training for. And once participating in the activity, the training becomes exhilarating. I enjoy running because I know what it feels like to be successful in races. I also know that without practice racing would no longer be pleasant. If I raced without practicing, I would never want to run again. Truthfully, when an individual doesn't know what racing feels like and he is just basing it off of having to run the mile in P.E., he cannot judge running. It would be similar to judging a book by its cover. We have all been taught that it is not fair.

Running weaves itself into my life tremendously. It is the one thing I look forward to taking part in every day. Not only is running an excellent hobby to carry out, it can be very useful in life, too. In my life, running has proved itself propitiously in various different ways. For one thing, it teaches patience. While waiting on the starting line of races, you must learn to be patient and cope with the anxiety of the situation. Physical toughness is necessary in running for the obvious reasons. If one is not physically fit, it is rare that he will be able to run and succeed in the sport of Cross Country. Apart from physical endurance, running helps the individual with mentality. He must have a different outlook on everything. Without the positive outlook, runners would give up whenever the going got tough (which is pretty much every day). This is why good runners do not give up easily in life as well; they have been trained to persevere no matter how challenging things may seem.

In the end, life is a race; we get to the start and everyone is nervous. No one knows if it will be okay and everyone is hoping it runs as planned. But right when it starts, things are somewhat a blur. We are questioned mentally throughout the entire event, and somewhere in the middle we face some kind of challenge. And in the blink of an eye, it's completed.

Stockholm
Talicia Montoya

Sitting here in the void, I'm aware only of the mattress below me and the wall against my back. I can't tell whether it's day or night; you keep me locked in this room, trapped in the shadows. The time of day matters not in a situation such as mine.

The door creaks open, sounding like the scream of a demon. Previously, the only sounds in this vacuum were the breaths rattling in and out of my lungs. Light floods in, searing my deprived eyes, and my hands scrabble to offer protection.

You laugh; it's not demeaning, just amused. "What's wrong?" you say, your words slicing through the dim air. I can't answer; if I try, my voice will come out all wrong. I'm not sure whether I can handle knowing how much I've deteriorated since you first captured me.

"I brought you something special," you coo. Again, you've left the door open, but you know I can't escape, not in my withered state. I'm your flower; the flower you keep in the dark so only you can enjoy its beauty.

The mattress sinks down on one side; you sit on the edge of the bed. In the poor lighting, I can't see the details of your features, and the shadows playing across your face give you a frightening countenance. They obscure your mouth, your nose and your eyes. You're the demon. You cock your head after my lack of a response and say, "Don't you want your present?"

I shake my head, although I can't say the words: *I don't want anything from a monster born from fear.*

You reach your hand out toward me, and I yank back, trying to escape into the corner. "Come here," you say as you wrap your hand around my head. Your fingers tangle into my limp hair, pressing against my scalp while you pull me closer. "I'm not going to hurt you. I just want you to have this." You place a small round package on my lap, and I look down at it, shivering. Its diameter is no more than a foot long, and it's tied shut with a pale ribbon. In the dark, colors are near impossible to distinguish.

When I don't move, you put your hands over mine and guide them to the knot. You help me untie the ribbon and remove the lid. I can't breathe as you lift whatever was inside out of the box. It's a gorgeous garment made of diaphanous material—a nightgown. On me, it wouldn't reach past my thighs. The straps are thin, and the cut is a low scoop. The top of it is a sheer white, and the bottom is gossamer ebony.

Your voice is reverent as you say, "It's better than the ratty old T-shirt you sleep in. I thought you'd like it." You're waiting for me to say something, anything, a thank you, perhaps. You set it back down in its box and watch me process what this offering could possibly mean. I'm terrified you'll want to take me on this tiny bed. "Do you like it?" you ask, stroking the back of my hand. But I can't answer; I'm speechless. You take my silence as an affirmation. "Go ahead. Put it on."

Stunned, I give you a petrified glance. You're still smiling; your teeth glint like a knife winking in sunlight. "I won't look," you whisper as you press your leg against mine. I stiffen, revolted at your touch. "Promise." You stand and turn your back on me, just a silhouette standing in the doorway.

Hesitating, I turn away from you in case you lied about not peeking and pull my shirt over my head. You are right about the gown being better than what I'm currently wearing.

I wasn't dressed to go out and about when you took me. All I wanted to do was take out the trash and go back into my home to sleep. That's all, but no, you decided I couldn't do that. You decided I needed a liberal dose of chloroform and a one-way trip to your cave.

It's cold wearing no more than the new nightgown, and I'm reduced to hugging myself on the bed. "All done?" you ask, still standing in the doorway with your back to me. I refuse to speak, concentrating on keeping my teeth from chattering. You peek over your shoulder, possibly hoping I'm partially dressed despite your promise. "Oh good!" You clap your hands together and approach me once again. You wrap your arms around me and caress my hair with your fingertips.

It occurs to me how truly vulnerable I am in this outfit, how you can easily overpower me if you have the desire to do so. My heart races in my chest, and I need to escape this room. You can probably feel it pounding against my rib cage like a battering ram.

"You're beautiful," you say in my ear, "It makes me happy enough to burst."

I hope you explode. I hope you become no more than pink mist. I want to spit this at you; instead, I say in a hoarse voice, "Please don't."

You end our awkward hug and hold me out at arm's length. Your hands are large enough to cover both my shoulders. "Don't what?" you ask confused with my sudden decision to speak.

The words are bitter cough medicine in my mouth. "Don't hurt me," I whisper so quietly, I doubt you'll hear it.

The pressure on my shoulders lightens, and you laugh. "I'm not going to hurt you. Look," you let go of me and get off the bed, holding my sweats and T-shirt. "I won't touch you if that's what you want."

I can't look at you as I continue, "I want to go home."

"Can't let you do that," you say, wagging a finger at me.

"What are you going to do with me?" My voice gains more confidence with each syllable.

"Nothing, right now." You back out of the room—or is it a cell—and become another shadow. The light behind you makes your grin sinister and suggestive. "Good night." The door closes behind you, and the sound of the deadbolt locking is a gunshot in my ears.

The darkness envelops me once again.

Day four, or is it five? I see colored flashes in the night. They put on a scintillating show. Some are floating orbs, dancing around with sparks in their centers. Others are like fireworks on the fourth of July, explosions of light chasing away the total blackness. They remind me of going to see fireworks with my mom and dad when I was no older than fourteen. My cheeks feel wet now.

You came up behind me while I dropped the lid over the garbage can. You looked nice, a proper gentleman. All an act. "Excuse me," you said, tapping me on the shoulder, "I seemed to have dropped my keys, could you please help me find them?" I didn't think it was strange how you approached me; there was no danger in your sheepish smile. It was almost as if you were embarrassed to ask for help. All an act. As soon as I turned away to aid your search, you clapped a damp rag over my mouth and nose. Struggling was pointless; you were too strong for my petite frame. All an act.

The color dissipates, overcome with shadows, and I remember reading somewhere how the brain will make you see things in total darkness. My eyes are open; I can hear the tiny clicks of my blinking. They're open, but they see nothing.

I crawl under the bed. Lying on top, I feel too out in the open. The comfort of having something over me is a small win, but every victory in here is as necessary as the absent sun. The sun I may never see again.

A hand jostles me and a voice says, "Time to wake up." It's gentle and full of love. I'm fifteen, and my mom is trying to get me up for school. My arms cover my eyes, and I roll over wanting to return to sleep. "Wake up, my flower."

I'm twenty-two again, and it's your hand on my shoulder. It was your voice full of misguided love. My stomach gives an unpleasant *urk*, and for a moment, I think I might be sick on you. I try turning away, but your hand wraps around my wrist.

"Time to get up, silly," you say as you pull me out from under the bed. "I made breakfast special for you." There's a tray sitting on the bed. From what I can make out in the dark it holds a glass filled to the brim, a plate with a stack of what might be waffles or pancakes, and a fork.

I briefly toy with the notion of using the fork to stab you and escape, but it'd be for naught. You'd still catch up with me. I'm slow to stand up, and I feel goosebumps rise on my bare arms and legs. It's not from the cold in the room. It's because of the cold in your heart.

"Cold?" you ask as though it's not obvious. A blanket slides off the bed; you drape it over my shoulders. "Better?" I shiver while you rub my shoulders through the blanket.

Biting my bottom lip, I think, maybe, you'll let me go if I'm nice. "Yes," I say in a soft voice.

You smile and pull me onto your lap. "I made blueberry pancakes. They're your favorite," you say, sending another chill rushing down my spine. They *are* my favorite, but you shouldn't know that.

I feel the rough fabric of jeans under my legs; your muscles are tense beneath. You don't hand the fork to me; instead, you cut off a piece from the warm stack and hold it in front of my face. I try not to consider the possibility of you drugging the food as I part my lips and obligingly take it in my mouth. "Good," comes your voice close to my ear. My compliance pleases you, and you continue to feed me. It's humiliating, but I'm willing to do whatever I must if it results in freedom.

Soon, the plate is empty, and you're pressing the cup to my mouth. "Just a little more," you say. "Finish your breakfast." I swallow my hesitation and finish drinking the juice in less than a minute. I feel it slosh in my stomach and feel nauseous again. "Very good," you say rubbing my back now.

I slide off your lap and collapse on the bed, exhausted from the effort of not fighting you. I never knew doing nothing could take so much out of a person.

"I'll be right back." You leave the room, locking the door behind you.

It's frightening having nothing but the darkness. I'm gasping, breaths hitching, lungs burning. It's hard to breathe; the air is viscous like syrup. Dizzy, I fall off the mattress and wind up lying on the floor with my arms wrapped around my stomach. It hurts to move, and I can't do anything but remain motionless.

This is how you find me when you return. "Oh, flower," you say. A thump on the floor, and you're kneeling next to me. Your hands smooth my hair. You lift me up, hugging me against your warm body. I know I shouldn't let you hold me, but it's better than the arms of the indifferent shadows. You don't say my name: just "flower" over and over. It's like a lullaby and soothes me.

I'm no longer gasping and sobbing. The only sounds I make are muffled sniffles. The rocking is calming, and eventually, you put me back on the bed and straighten my nightgown. "It's okay, flower, I'm here." You're here and you're the only other person I've seen in a week. Yes, you're here, and so am I.

I don't know how many days it's been since I first vanished from the outside. All I know is the darkness and you. You come again, this time with offerings of brownies and ice cream. We're meant to share, though you've only brought a single plate and spoon. "My flower," you say. Always "my flower" and nothing else.

The brownies are fresh; warmer than the icy box I live in. You're warm, too. I think it's nice to have someone else with me, even if it is *you*.

You haven't done anything to me yet, save your caresses

and cooing. It makes me wonder what's in store, what venomous cobra lies in the shadows, biding its time. You say you won't touch me if I don't want you to. I shouldn't want you to touch me, but there's no one else.

The bowl is soon empty as you slip the final spoonful of vanilla ice cream (again, my favorite) into my mouth. Putting down the spoon, you fold your lips over mine.

It's like kissing a dead man; your lips aren't warm like the rest of you. Shoving you away with both hands on your chest, I retch. You don't do it again. You just sit there watching me dry heave. Trying to breathe in the thick darkness, I gasp for air.

And you're there patting my back with one hand while your other hand holds my hair out of my face. It's a natural gesture to do if a loved one is going to be sick, but you're not allowed to love me. Everything about this is wrong, twisted, and disturbing.

Nothing comes up, and I lean back against the wall, shivering.

"Oh, flower," you whisper in my ear as you stroke the damp hair from my feverish brow. Maybe, I am getting sick. "I'm sorry. I thought you were ready."

Your words chill me more than the shadows. "*I thought you were ready.*" *When will you think I'm ready for more than a stolen kiss?* This question makes me gag again, and instead of letting me bend over the bed, you pull me against your broad chest.

We remain in this position for minutes—or they could be hours, maybe, even days—and I close my eyes. If I imagine you're my dad protecting a ten-year-old me from nightmares, I can stand it. I keep my eyes closed and breathe in the scent of (my dad's) your familiar musk. It's not entirely unpleasant, and therein lies the problem, because I sort of like it.

I'm sitting on the cold floor; it's hard and uncomfortable, but I don't mind. The darkness doesn't bother me anymore, and I think I'm getting used to it. I think I'm getting used to you. My ear is pressed against the door, listening for your footsteps, waiting for you.

Here comes the distinct *tap, tap, tap* of your shoes on the floor. I stand and step back a couple of feet. The door swings in and there you are. The light you bring makes me shrink away, but it's not potent enough to keep me from you.

"Hello, flower," you say, closing the door. We're plunged back in wonderful darkness. "I'm sorry. I don't have anything special for you today."

It's okay, because all I need is comfort and a companion. I crawl onto the bed and wait for you to make the first move. Closing my eyes, I hear you cross the room and join me. You take my hand in yours and stroke it with the soft pads of your fingers. We don't speak a word in those silent seconds, but, somehow, we manage to say everything.

"Flower, I've been thinking." You pause as though expecting a response. "It's been three months, and I think I've waited long enough."

The only part of this I hear is "three months," and I'm finding it hard to believe it's been that long.

Your breath tickles my cheek; it smells like a peppermint candy. I sense your face is only centimeters from mine, and you're letting me make the decision.

I'm aware of your hands on mine, your body sharing this cage with me, the warmth coming from your mouth, and most of all, the darkness sliding inside my chest. My heart flutters as if it knows the gravity of the situation.

Not thinking, not feeling, I close the distance between us. You are pleased. Our kiss lasts a few seconds, though it feels like several minutes. We break apart. You're panting, and I can't breathe. My lungs are pieces of ice in my chest; the shadows replace them.

Your hands trail from my hands to comb through my hair, then down and around. Your arms are on either side of my neck, and your hands rest on my back. Your dangling fingertips give me the chills, and I fight to conceal my trembling.

"Oh, flower," you practically moan. You press your forehead against mine; your warm skin banishes my cold. "I'm so happy. So happy I could burst." The statement echoes your earliest one.

I, too, feel I could burst, yet, I don't know the name of this new feeling. My brain tries to provide the appropriate words, but none of them fit. Joy...disgust...pleasure... condemnation... They're all wrong.

Or, maybe, they're not wrong, but this is.

And now, I'm crying, sobbing, gasping, choking. My hands tear at my hair; my nails claw at my face. You do nothing except sit there and watch me break down from within.

I'm numb, not feeling anything while simultaneously feeling everything. It hurts my scalp to pull my hair, but it hurts more to not know what I'm feeling. It hurts to cut trenches in my cheeks, but it hurts more to know I kissed you. The physical pain is bad, but the mental confusion is absolute agony.

You wait for me to take a hitching, excruciating breath, and it rips my throat all the way to my lungs. Your hand on my shoulder is comforting but sickening. Your gentle name "flower" degrades me each time you say it.

I don't know when you get up and leave, but I'm left alone whimpering and groaning on this tiny bed. The bed on which you'll want to take me. The bed on which I might let you. This makes me start screaming again, because I don't know what I'm doing. Don't know what I've done. Don't know what I'll do.

When you return, I'm hiding under the bed. It catches you off guard, and you kneel down beside it. "What are you doing under there, my flower?"

Now, I'm not only "flower" but I'm *your* "flower". I turn my face from you, feeling the dried tears on my cheeks.

"What's wrong?" Your voice is so convincing, I almost crawl into your lap for comfort, but I remind myself it's all an act. Your hand grips my wrist as it has done in the past, and you drag me out into the open. "My flower, why are you crying?"

I don't have the energy to fight you as you pull me to your chest like you did before. "Flower?" you whisper into my ear with your arms tight around my body like binding ropes. "I know what can make you feel better. I know what can make both of us feel better." With this, I know you're done waiting.

You lift me to the bed and kiss the fresh tears off my face. Your hands are elsewhere, tugging at the gown, the gift you gave me. My body is limp and frozen, my limbs too heavy to move. I'm a statue carved out of ice. Your hands, arms, and legs are warm like fire.

I can't fight you.
(don't want to)
I can't fight the night.
(don't want to)
I can't fight the shadows inside me.
(don't want to)
And I fade into blackness, nothingness, emptiness.
I fade into the dark.

The Case of the Missing Umbrella
Natasha Culbreth

The audience waited silently in the warm California sun. Their cameras and phones, held high into the air, collectively fought for space. These objects conjointly reflected the sunlight, creating a sea of glare. Although growing impatient, the crowd stood a respectful distance away from the main attraction. All eyes were focused on a intricate sand painting in the center of the courtyard. Crimson and gold robed monks were its creators and guardians. A low throaty hum started, filling the packed area. The bellow and chime of primitive horns and bells followed. Multicolored prayer flags strung across the quad trembled in a sudden gust of soft wind. Many people in the crowd pressed to get closer. Every inch of occupiable space was filled with an attentive body. Koi ponds and oriental stone sculptures randomly punctured the filled area. A chill ran its cold fingers down my back as the hum reverberated.

As I watched this spectacle safely from a perch high above the crowd, I marveled at the beauty and the intricacy of the mandala. Vibrant hues of blue, green, yellow, red, and white swirled and danced in the work, creating a vibrant geometry in this delicate transient creation. The humming was drawn out and haunting. There was something otherworldly and frightening, yet at the same time, captivating about it. Movement on the stone fence before me caught my eye. Slowly, a large roach revealed itself. Its glistening body rested in close proximity to me. I regarded it silently as the humming continued. A pigeon then took roost atop the slanted roof to my left, its gaze fixed on the demonstration. Soon, a wasp joined the duo, dancing unnoticed above the heads of the crowd. The continuous vibration of the drone had awakened the creatures who inhabit this concrete complex. A sudden wind strummed the roach's antenna.

A monk stepped forward, lowering his head as he ran his hand through the sand which shifted like water. The colors and shapes warped. We were witnesses to the destruction of a world. He tossed the sand, rendering the labors of the monks' work a mass of gray. I descended from my safe haven, delving into the sea of bodies that were jostling for the now neutral colored remnants of the painting. The monks graciously and calmly distributed it. The wind caused the colorful *lung ta* to flutter once more. Suddenly, rising over the blissful murmur of the spectators, came the harsh cry of a man.

"DO NOT TAKE THIS UNHOLY SAND!"

Most ignored the voice, others looked toward the entrance of the small courtyard with curiosity.

"Do not take this DANGEROUS sand into your homes, it will attract the evil eye! You will DIE!"

"Now, I *really* want some magic sand!" I laughed. My mother was trailing behind me as we slowly waded through the chortling crowd. The Tibetan monks, who relied heavily on their translator, were unaware of the context of the intrusion and continued to diligently hand out the sacred relics.

A woman, attempting to dive through the crowd, announced informally,

"We're terribly sorry about this! Someone, *please*, call security!"

"The crazies always come out of the woodwork before election season!" a woman commented cynically to her companions. When I finally reached the table, I was greeted by a smiling monk who cordially offered me a packet of the "cursed" sand. Outside of the museum, a police car was parked. An officer was questioning witnesses as a helicopter spun nosily overhead. We joined the exiting crowd who, for the most part, moved in tandem down the street unperturbed by the scenario. They behaved as typical urban dwellers, unruffled by such eccentricities.

We meandered along the street, gazing into the windows of storefronts as we made our way to our vehicle. Feeling we had satisfied our spiritual needs, we sought to edify our physical cravings. The dry heat made us yearn for Mediterranean fare. Visions of freshly cut shawarma and thick slices of honey coated baklava propelled us to a local race track where a Greek church was sponsoring a festival.

As we entered the festivity, our olfactory senses were assaulted by the aroma of herb roasted lamb. We entered a lively village composed of Delphi blue and white striped tents. Vendors hawked a variety of Greek themed products. Some offered wine tastings, others purveyed olive oil and goat cheese. Music emanated from a large central tent where children garbed in native Aegean dress danced. Girls outnumbered boys as arm in arm they swayed in unison to the enervating music. At one point the boys energetically leaped onto each others shoulders, creating a human pyramid. After enjoying this spectacle for a few minutes, we moved on and gravitated toward a dinner queue. We were pleasantly surprised by the heaping piles of fragrant Moussaka offered by volunteer church members. We dined alfresco, savoring the warm orange glow of the sky as the sun disappeared behind the mountains. By the time we exited the gala, the moonless night was black.

As we navigated our vehicle through the pitch darkness, we were startled by a strange apparition. There was an eerie glow in one corner of the vast asphalt parking lot. Like a scene from a dystopian film, multiple welders were creating sparks as they worked on top of steel freight containers. In the darkness, we struggled to discern the identity of some strange shapes that were on the edge of the property close to us. We repositioned our vehicle, focusing our headlights on the mysterious objects. To our surprise, the forms were vintage train cars. Our attempts to illuminate the objects attracted the attention of a security guard, who swiftly approached, seeking to send us on our way.

"You can't park here! The exit is the other way! If you—"

"What are they filming?" I interrupted, eagerly leaning from my window.

"The Lone Ranger."

I masked my amazement with a grin. What a grand coincidence that we would happen upon the set of a Johnny Depp movie.

"You can come tomorrow to watch the filming if you like, they'll be here all day," the man responded encouragingly. He immediately interjected, "But you can't park here now!"

As we drove away, excitement swelled in me; I gleefully contemplated my chances of seeing my favorite actor in person. It was truly an extraordinary, once in a lifetime opportunity!

We arrived home in excellent spirits after our marathon of activity. My aunt who had decided to make a surprise visit was waiting for us. The remnants of the long hot day were palpable once we opened the door to our small abode. Seeking more circulation, we immediately flung open all the doors and windows in a mad frenzy. My mother stopped in her tracks when she opened the French doors leading to the back terrace. We all gazed in that direction, taking in the view. The kaleidoscope of colored lights from the tall buildings downtown sparkled and danced before us. Something in the picturesque scene was missing. The curious emptiness clawed at me until I heard my mother say,

"Where did the patio umbrella go?"

The soft wind rustled the bushes below the porch. I looked up in disbelief, the sky was bare above me, cold stars twinkled in the umbrella's stead.

"It has to be somewhere, maybe, you took it down and forgot?" offered my aunt.

"I always leave it up to keep the sun off the porch."

We stood there twisting our bodies in every which way, hoping to locate the missing object.

"It was a cool umbrella…" we explained to my perplexed aunt who sat there slumped in a chair, weary after the long drive to our house.

"It had solar powered LED lights. We thought it would be a handy thing to have during power outages."

"Maybe someone who was having an outdoor party saw it and decided to borrow it," my aunt conjectured.

"We usually leave a lot of things laying about in even more accessible places, and no one ever touches them," my mother mused.

"The neighbor's getting their roof redone, perhaps, it was the workers," I volunteered.

"I don't know how they would access the porch since there is no entry except through the house," my mother noted.

"It's not hard to climb—," my aunt ventured. "Wait, what's this?"

My aunt knelt down and revealed a circular piece of plastic. It was the apparatus that contained the solar panel for the umbrella.

"Don't touch it!" I cried. "It might have fingerprints on it!"

"It must have fallen off when they were taking the umbrella away," my mother stated as she moved toward the phone.

Half an hour later, our living room was illuminated by the flashing lights of a police car in the street. Two local cops strode across our lawn and approached our house. They made their way into our tiny dining room. Their stature seemed to dwarf the miniscule house. We wearily showed them the scene of the crime, explaining our predicament. They examined the porch, peered vertically and horizontally, and then one of them nonchalantly picked up the plastic rig we had found, obviously unconcerned about contaminating "forensic evidence."

"We believe it may had been stolen. It may seem odd to

take a patio umbrella, but this one was a bit unusual," my mother reported to them.

"What about your *kids*? Do you think they may have done something with it?" one of the officers questioned.

"They were with me all day."

"What about their *friends*?" The officer pointed the beam of his heavy flashlight toward two eyes that peered through a slit in the adjoining door as my brother slid backward, an expression of guilt pained his face, as if he had committed some crime. We shrugged in response. The officers then peered into the dark abyss of our backyard.

"What about that bicycle out there?" The two visitors focused their flashlights on the yard full of miscellaneous items that we had carelessly strewn through the course of the blazing rainless summer. They concurred that the culprits might have been the roofers, since they were the only strangers in the area at the time. They would have had a vantage point into our back porch and would have been able to see us leave.

One of the officers inscribed all the pertinent details of the case onto a form attached to a clipboard. They were not optimistic that there would be a satisfactory resolution. However, they thought the petty nature of the crime was indicative that it was one of opportunity and the culprits probably would not be back. Nevertheless, my mother was not consoled. We felt violated. Someone had destroyed our sense of security. I stood there and had an inkling that this disturbing event could potentially disrupt my hopes of returning to the movie set and obtaining a glimpse of Johnny Depp on the morrow.

That night, despite the heat, we felt compelled to lock down the house, but we could not bear the loss of the slight breeze that entered through the back patio doors. I took out my sleeping bag and found a position as sentry at the base of the doors. The moon washed the room with cold light.

"Are you sure you want to sleep out here?" my mother asked.

"I'll be fine, I doubt there is another robber hiding out there in the shadows." I sunk down in weariness into my makeshift bed.

I woke a short time later to find my mother frantically closing the shutters of the French doors.

"What happened?" I murmured groggily

"I thought I saw the motion detector light go on." She continued to secure the doors, attempting to restore a sense of sanctuary.

In the bright sunlight of the morning, the world appeared to return to normal. My harried aunt packed up and rushed out the door for a professional meeting. My brother, who associated the arrival of the police with his phobia that Homeland Security may have been alerted when he borrowed a tome about the history of the FBI from the local library, decided it was now safe to come out of his room. My mother, however, was missing. I ventured outside, went down the back steps, and found her rummaging through storage containers in the garage.

"What are you looking for?"

"The safe. I thought your father had a small safe stored down here. I'm worried that perhaps it was stolen as well. I still can't believe that someone would go through all that trouble for a patio umbrella..."

Feeling that I had no way to genuinely assist her in the search, I started back toward the house. As I was climbing the stairway, something drew my attention to the roof.

"Look, up there!" my mother cried as she pointed upward. To my astonishment the umbrella lay upended on a flat portion of the roof. We studied the spectacle silently, puzzled by the sight.

"How on earth did it get up there? There was not a lot of wind yesterday, and it doesn't have wings," my mother laughed.

"I'll help you get the ladder," I sighed.

We balanced the ladder against the wall that provided access to the roof. The two of us stood there, trying to determine what our next move would be. Although the roof was flat, and easy to walk on, there was a problem with the height. The house is on a slope, so the back portion is suspended in a way that the roof is equivalent to three stories—not one story, which is the actual configuration of the structure. My father, who was out of town, often goes up there, however, neither of us felt comfortable with the prospect of that kind of elevation. The irony of our situation was not lost on us. We could call the roofers. They would not be intimated by the height. But we felt we were not deserving of their assistance after our unsubstantiated accusations. Therefore, justice was served—one of us would have to suffer the consequences. My mother, with a blanched face, gingerly started to mount the ladder. As she approached the final two steps, acrophobia took over, she could go no further. She suggested that I search for some sort of long stick that would enable her to wrestle the umbrella free of its lodgings. I returned with the hooked rod of a tree pruner. She slowly pulled the umbrella toward the edge. When it was near the precipice, she quickly dismounted before the umbrella knocked her off the ladder. With clenched teeth, I watched the inverted parasol skid off the roof and land with a crash on the concrete patio floor, narrowly missing the two of us.

"It's a little banged up," my mother noted, dolefully picking up the mass of misshapen metal and canvas.

"Nothing a little duct tape won't fix... I guess that solves the case of the missing umbrella, though I am still curious how it managed to get on the roof." As I spoke, a sudden wind caressed my cheek and the lace curtains hanging by the patio entrance fluttered.

"Maybe, it *was* the wind."

When my mother called the sheriff station to cancel the report, she and the desk sergeant shared a hearty laugh. He was on duty the night before and remembered the unusual call. He, too, was incredulous, because he had not noticed any aberrant weather conditions the prior day. Although the mystery was now formally solved, I decided to cancel the anticipated excursion to find Johnny Depp. By mid-morning it was apparent the blazing heat of the previous day was going to continue. Obtaining an autograph from this mega star while standing in the midst of a sea of a hundred and thirty degree asphalt seemed highly unlikely.

Later that day I noticed a sizable bite mark upon my leg. This was curious to me, as I did not recall having been in contact with any sort of creature that would have produced such an impression. Once again, I felt the whisper of a breeze. It eerily ran down my neck, causing me to wonder. Was this the work of the Santa Anas, winds that are notorious for creating conditions during which, as Raymond Chandler famously stated in the opening of his crime story, *Red Wind*, "anything can happen?" Perhaps, the culprit was a mischievous gremlin who had suddenly taken residence in our household, *or*, maybe, the warning at the mandala ceremony did have some credence in an oblique way. I ruminated that life had certainly been unusual since I had acquired a few grains of sand.

The Courageous Bear
Amaya Hunsberger

A long time ago, deep within the forest, there lived a small tribe of people. Their chief was a good man, a brave warrior, and a loving father. His daughter was fragile and sweet and loved by all who met her.

She enjoyed spending her days out in the open and marveling at the beauty of nature. Some days, her exploring took her past a cave inhabited by a bear. She would smile and say hello before continuing on her outing.

One day, while picking wild flowers from a nearby stream, a hungry wolf crept up behind her. He had been watching the little girl, just waiting for the perfect moment to pounce. As she was turning around, she was startled to see the creature looming over her, and screamed. The bear, a short distance down the river, heard her cry and came running. Seeing the wolf about to attack the child, he knocked the wolf off his feet. They engaged in a fierce battle until the bear prevailed and approached the girl.

"Oh, do not kill me!" she pleaded, still sobbing. He spoke gently to her, "Come with me, dear one. Climb on my back, and I'll take you to your village; there is no need to fear me." They traveled in silence until they reached the gates of her village. After climbing off the bear's back, she rushed through the doors into her father's arms and, without waiting for a thank you, the bear quietly lumbered off.

www.ingramcontent.com/pod-product-compliance
Lightning Source LLC
Chambersburg PA
CBHW070023260626
47159CB00005B/1933